SUCCESSFUL GARDENING
THE INDOOR GARDEN

Staff for Successful Gardening (U.S.A.)
Editor: Carolyn T. Chubet

Contributors
Editor: Thomas Christopher
Art Editor: Joan Gramatte
Editorial Assistant: Troy Dreier
Consulting Editor: Lizzie Boyd (U.K.)
Consultant: Dora Galitzki
Copy Editor: Sue Heinemann
Art Assistant: Antonio Mora

READER'S DIGEST GENERAL BOOKS
Editor in Chief: John A. Pope, Jr.
General Books Editor, U.S.: Susan Wernert Lewis
Affinity Directors: Will Bradbury, Jim Dwyer, Kaari Ward
Art Director: Evelyn Bauer
Editorial Director: Jane Polley
Research Director: Laurel A. Gilbride
Group Art Editors: Robert M. Grant, Joel Musler
Copy Chief: Edward W. Atkinson
Picture Editor: Marion Bodine
Head Librarian: Jo Manning

Library of Congress Cataloging in Publication Data

The indoor garden.
      p.   cm. — (Successful gardening)
    ISBN 0-89577-684-7
    1. House plants.   2. House plants — Pictorial works.   3. Indoor
gardening.   I. Reader's Digest Association.   II. Series.
SB419.I49   1995
635.9'65—dc20   94-35382

Opposite: Rex begonias are among the most spectacular foliage plants.
Their large, heart-shaped leaves display stunning color
combinations and markings.

Overleaf: A window display of foliage plants is brightened by the
addition of a red-fruited annual winter cherry.

THE READER'S DIGEST ASSOCIATION, INC.
Pleasantville, New York / Montreal

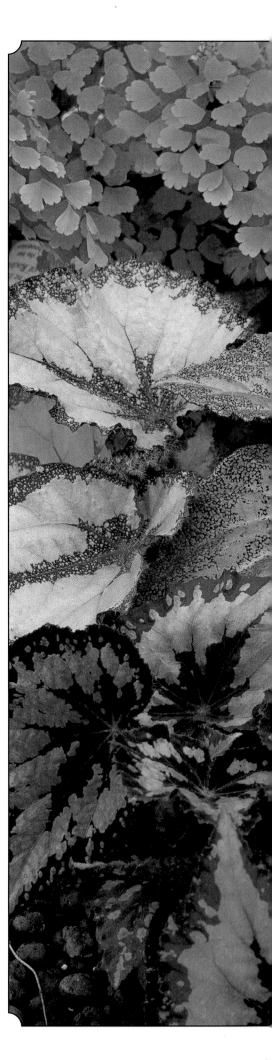

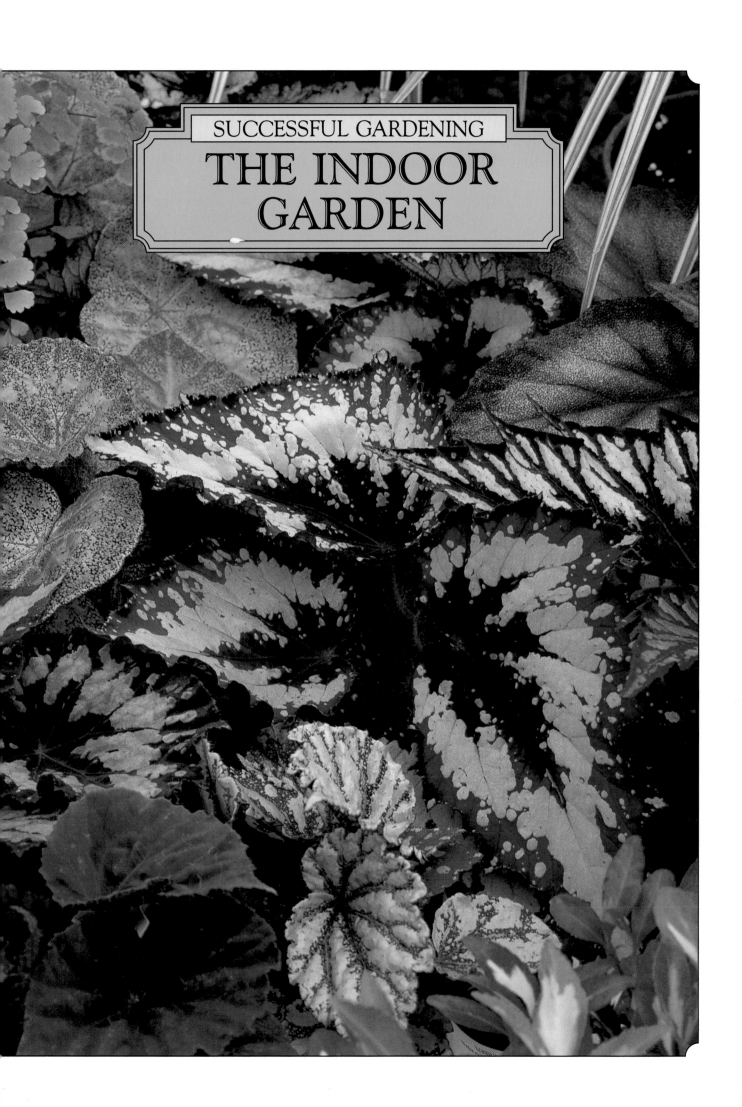

SUCCESSFUL GARDENING

THE INDOOR
GARDEN

CONTENTS

Caring for houseplants

Identifying houseplants

Decorating with plants

Unusual houseplants

Colorful plants Crotons, caladiums, and bright red poinsettias need good light and constant temperatures.

Caring for houseplants

Indoor plants depend entirely on their owners to meet their soil, water, light, air, and heat requirements. Although the majority of indoor plants cannot tolerate outdoor winter conditions, they do not need hothouse treatment either — more houseplants are killed by overzealous attention than by neglect.

Houseplants' basic needs vary enormously, depending on their origins. For example, foliage plants from steamy tropical rain forests differ greatly from cacti, which grow naturally in arid deserts, where hot days alternate with cold nights. Such differences must be taken into consideration when caring for houseplants.

No plant will survive in complete shade, but bright sun reflected through glass can be just as harmful. Good air circulation is essential, but drafts can be lethal. A compromise between such extremes suits most indoor plants, and as potted plants can readily be moved from one spot to another, it should be easy to find the most suitable site. The majority adapt surprisingly well to the artificial conditions found in the home, and as long as houseplants are provided with adequate light, water, and food they will develop steadily. Their well-being can be increased by meeting their individual needs for humidity, minimum temperatures, and a winter rest.

Although poor health may be caused by a few pests and diseases, it is more often the result of poor growing conditions, which can usually be improved. With regular care, you can make your indoor garden as striking as any outdoor garden.

Plant window Trailing, climbing, and upright foliage plants display a diversity of shapes and colors.

HOUSEPLANT CARE

Indoor plants vary in their specific needs, but certain basic conditions are essential if they are to thrive and remain healthy.

All plants have the same basic requirements — air, light, water, nutrients, humidity, and a suitable temperature range — although individual species vary enormously in the quantity and quality of these needs. The balance must be just right if a plant is to flourish in the artificial conditions inside a home. A knowledge of how and where the plant grows in the wild can help in deciding how it ought to be grown indoors. It's always best to choose plants that favor a particular home environment, rather than trying to alter conditions to suit a particular plant.

Air and airflow

Plants breathe, just like animals, but through pores in their leaf surfaces. They do not compete for air with animals during the day, since they breathe in carbon dioxide, rather than oxygen, to use in their food-making process. At the same time, they breathe out

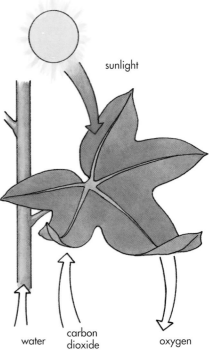

HOW PLANTS USE AIR

sunlight

water   carbon dioxide   oxygen

1 In daytime carbon dioxide is absorbed through pores on the underside of the leaf, and oxygen is released.

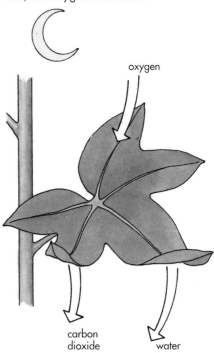

oxygen

carbon dioxide   water

2 At night the process is reversed: oxygen is absorbed, and carbon dioxide and water vapor are given off. The daytime process of producing food, or photosynthesis, requires sunlight plus water from the soil, while the conversion of food into plant energy — respiration — can be carried out in total darkness.

◀ **Indoor plants** In spite of their varying cultural needs, many tender and exotic plants, grown for foliage or flowers, will adapt to indoor conditions. Light is the most important factor for their continual well-being.

oxygen. At night, this process is reversed — small amounts of oxygen are used up and carbon dioxide is breathed out. Thus a constant supply of fresh, oxygen-rich air is not essential; many plants will thrive in the closed environment of a bottle garden or terrarium. However, there must be a balance with other essential conditions.

Far more important than freshness is the flow of air. Stagnant air can create an increase in temperature and humidity. Although these last two conditions may, by themselves, enhance a plant's health, in combination with poor air circulation they encourage fungal diseases such as botrytis, especially when plants are grown very close together. Drafts, too, may damage plants — causing leaf curl, yellowing, brown tips or edges, and sudden leaf fall. Don't open the window next to a house-

plant when outside temperatures are dramatically lower than those indoors. Equally damaging is an accumulation of gases toxic to plants, such as those that may result from the use of kerosene heaters.

Light

No plant will grow properly if it lacks sufficient light. Energy from sunlight is absorbed by the green pigment chlorophyll in the leaves and used as the fuel for converting carbon dioxide (from the surrounding air) and water into essential food substances. Most plants do not "feed" as animals do, but instead manufacture their own food.

Flowering plants need more light than foliage plants, since flower formation uses up a lot of energy. (Flowers are a plant's reproductive organs.)

Foliage plants native to deep

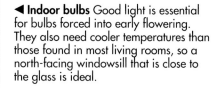

◀ **Indoor bulbs** Good light is essential for bulbs forced into early flowering. They also need cooler temperatures than those found in most living rooms, so a north-facing windowsill that is close to the glass is ideal.

▼ **Mobile plant stand** Indoor flowering plants generally need the best possible light, though on summer days they are liable to sun scorch. A plant stand on casters makes it easy to move plants in and out of diffused light.

Day length
The length of daylight is as important to some plants as light intensity. Poinsettias are short-day plants — red bracts form only if they receive 10 hours of light with at least 14 hours of uninterrupted darkness (a long night) every day for 8 weeks.

jungles, such as philodendrons, monsteras, and aglaonemas, are able to survive in fairly low levels of light. They often have very dark green leaves saturated with chlorophyll, so they can make maximum use of what little light there is. Usually slow-growing, they rarely flower in the home but are excellent for less well lit corners. With a slow "metabolism" in low light, they also use up less water and need watering less frequently than flowering plants do.

Plants with variegated leaves, such as spider plant (*Chlorophytum*) and wandering Jew (*Tradescantia*), have very little or no chlorophyll in the pale leaf regions and therefore less ability to absorb light, so they require brighter positions than all-green plants. So, too, do plants with entirely pale leaves, but there is another important consideration here — such leaves are often soft and easily scorched by direct sun shining through glass.

In the Northern Hemisphere south-facing windows are often too bright for all but cacti and flowering plants, unless summer sun is diffused by sheer curtains, blinds, or outdoor foliage. (In the Southern Hemisphere the sun's orientation is reversed.) Plants set in an east- or west-facing window, however, will receive sunlight only when the sun is at its coolest, in the morning or late afternoon — so these are usually ideal positions for sun-loving plants. Bright but filtered light is the most suitable for the majority of sun-loving plants.

Partial shade is found near a north-facing window or in any area several steps back from a sunny window. Areas well away from any window will have continuous shade — conditions suited only to certain foliage plants. As a rule of thumb, if there isn't enough natural light during the day to read a newspaper comfortably without turning on the electric lights, there isn't enough light to grow plants.

When light comes from just one source — from a single window, for instance — leaves turn to face it, leaning away from the room interior. To counteract this, turn the pots regularly. Young flower buds may, however, object to sudden exposure to stronger light and fall off.

Rooms with white or pale-colored walls are obviously much brighter than those decorated in darker shades. White walls in particular are effective, as they reflect some of the available light back onto the plants.

Temperature
As many houseplants come from tropical climates, some people assume that they need equally high temperatures when grown in the home. This is certainly not the case. Temperatures much above 75°F (24°C) are acceptable only when daylight hours are very long, light is very strong, and humidity is near the saturation point. Most of us do not live in such environments.

At the other end of the scale, few houseplants can thrive in temperatures much below 55°F (13°C). The best temperature and the acceptable temperature range vary according to the particular plant species, together with the associated conditions of light, air, water, and humidity (see chart below).

A moderate drop in temperature at night, 5°-10°F (3°-5.5°C), is beneficial to most plants, but it is important to avoid sudden and dramatic fluctuations. The temperature in a sunny room may soar on a clear winter day, and if heating is turned down at night, a drop of up to 20°F (11°C) is

TEMPERATURE REQUIREMENTS		
Plant type	Growth	Temperature range
Ferns	Active	65°-75°F/18°-24°C
	Dormant	55°-65°F/13°-18°C
Hardy palms	Active	59°-75°F/15°-24°C
	Dormant	45°-75°F/7°-24°C
Tender palms	Active	59°-75°F/15°-24°C
	Dormant	55°-75°F/13°-24°C
Orchids/Succulents	All year	65°-75°F/18°-24°C
Desert cacti	Active	65°-75°F/18°-24°C
	Dormant	39°-45°F/4°-7°C
Jungle cacti	All year	59°-75°F/15°-24°C
Other plants	Active	59°-75°F/15°-24°C
	Dormant	55°-65°F/13°-18°C

Note: Normal comfortable living room temperature is 65°-75° F/18°-24° C.

common, which can be quite damaging to plants. Also, the temperature in a hallway may fluctuate widely when exterior doors are opened.

To minimize these effects, take sensitive plants off windowsills at night, especially during the coldest periods in winter. In addition, seal out drafts as much as possible. Heavy curtains will do much to reduce nighttime heat loss through glass.

Humidity
Water is essential to all plants,

11

INCREASING AIR HUMIDITY

1 Mist plants daily with a hand sprayer, using tepid water. Allow time for the moisture to evaporate before nightfall.

2 Put pebbles or coarse grit in the saucer, and keep this layer wet — but never let the pot stand in water.

3 Sink the whole pot within a second, larger one, and pack the cavity with water-retaining peat or sphagnum moss.

4 Stand the pot on a block within its saucer, so that a small pool of water can be maintained below pot level.

5 Special humidifiers can be hung on radiators, improving the room humidity — especially just above radiators.

6 Small plants that thrive in very high humidity are grown most successfully in a bottle garden.

whether they are native to the driest desert or the wettest rain forest. Air humidity is a general environmental factor related to temperature and is essential to plant health. In technical terms it is the relative humidity — measured on a range of 0-100 percent, completely dry to fully saturated with water vapor — that needs checking. Cold winter air quickly becomes saturated with moisture, but as the temperature rises, its capacity to absorb water vapor increases. As a result, when cold air is artificially heated in wintertime, its relative humidity automatically drops and it may turn from moist to dry. For a pleasant indoor atmosphere, for people and plants alike, 40-60 percent air humidity is ideal.

The only way to find out the exact humidity level of any room is to use a hygrometer. In a heated room with double-glazed windows and weather-stripped doors,

WHAT'S WRONG?

Light
❏ Spindly growth or no new growth at all — too little light.
❏ Leaves paler or smaller than normal (eventually turn yellow and fall) — too little light.
❏ Flowering plants fail to bloom — too little light.
❏ Variegated foliage turns all-green — too little light.
❏ Foliage wilts in peak light conditions (may shrivel and die) — too much direct sun; move sensitive plants away from direct sun, especially around midday, when the sun is hottest.
❏ Scorched brownish patches on leaves, especially on thick and succulent foliage — too much direct sunlight through glass.

Temperature
❏ Leaves rapidly turn yellow and/or fall off — sudden and extreme temperature fluctuation.
❏ Leaves curl up, then turn brown and fall off — temperature too low.

❏ Weak, spindly shoot growth despite suitable light conditions — temperature too high.
❏ Leaves at the base of plant wilt, then turn brown and crinkly at their edges, and finally fall off — temperature too high and light too poor.
❏ Flowers wither or fall off prematurely — temperature too high.
❏ Flower buds fail to develop — temperature too high and humidity too low.

Humidity
❏ Leaves become yellow along their edges, sometimes wilting — air too dry.
❏ Leaf tips turn brown and crinkly, and/or leaves fall off — air too dry.
❏ Flowers and buds die prematurely — air too dry.
❏ Powdery mildew appears on leaves, stems, flowers, or buds, often stunting growth — air too moist, together with poor ventilation and too high temperature.

the reading may frequently be as low as 15 percent humidity, which is as dry as in a desert.

The problem of dry air can be overcome with an automatically controlled electric humidifier to increase the overall indoor level of air moisture. The most effective remedies for plants are cultural ones. Growing plants in small groups creates a microclimate in which moisture evaporating from the potting soil accumulates within the mass of foliage. Airflow is decreased and therefore relative humidity is increased. Do not overcrowd plants, however, where the temperature is high and ventilation is poor, since this may encourage fungal diseases.

Routine care

More houseplants are killed by overwatering than by anything else. The amount of water to be given depends on the type of plant, the room temperature, and the time of year. Every plant also needs various nutrients in order to be able to grow satisfactorily. A newly purchased plant should have a supply of the necessary nutrients in the potting mixture, but eventually these must be replaced.

Watering

You need to know how much — and how often — to water each plant. The amount of water a plant requires depends to some extent on the natural environment of its country of origin; plants come from a wide variety of environments, from arid deserts to wet rain forests.

A cactus that would receive almost no water at all for much of the year in its desert home will require much less water in the living room than, say, a potted rush, which is used to marshlands. A fancy-leaved caladium *(Caladium × hortulanum)* resting in winter needs only enough water to prevent the tuber from shriveling, while a winter-flowering begonia has to be watered moderately throughout the winter months.

The environmental conditions under which a houseplant is grown also affect its needs. In hot, dry weather or in a well-heated room, a large amount of water is lost through the leaf pores and by evaporation from the potting soil. If hot sun shines directly on a potted plant, the evaporation and drying out of the soil will be rapid. In situations where temperatures are naturally cool, plants will lose much less moisture.

During the active growth period, developing leaves and flowers need their full ration of water. Yet when resting — after blooming or during the darker, cooler season of midwinter — the same plant may often be able to survive with very little. Whether it is active or resting, the more roots a plant has, the more rapidly it will use up water.

The type of container also influences the rate of water loss. Unglazed clay pots, for example, lose more water by evaporation than glazed ceramic or plastic types. The size of a plant relative to its container makes a difference too — as a rule, the larger the plant, the sooner the soil will dry out.

Finally, the type of potting mixture affects water requirements. Peat-based potting mixes hold less water than loam-based ones, and those with extra sand or perlite lose water faster than standard mixtures. Providing each type of plant with the appropriate potting mix — a sandy mix for cacti and an organically rich mix for African violets — is the best way to ensure that all plants get the amount of water that they prefer.

Above all, do not water by the calendar. Instead, inspect your plants daily, and water when the soil is dry.

◀ **Slow-release fertilizers** Granular plant foods are specially formulated to release the vital nutrients — nitrogen, phosphorus, and potassium — over several months. Blend them into the potting mixture, well away from the roots.

WATERING METHODS

1 For indoor use, choose a lightweight watering can with a long spout that can direct a gentle stream of water with reasonable accuracy. Apply water to the soil surface without wetting the foliage.

2 If dense foliage permits little or no free entry of water to the soil surface, or if the leaves are hairy or spread over the soil in a low rosette, water from below, but don't let the pots stand permanently in water.

3 Most bromeliads do not take up water through their roots, which are for anchorage only. Instead, they absorb water through their leaves, so keep the leaf rosette — which forms a reservoir — constantly filled.

Water quality Tap water is normally quite satisfactory for most houseplants. However, azaleas and other acid-loving plants such as camellias are likely to develop yellow leaves if they are permanently watered with hard (alkaline) water. So for these plants it is best to use rainwater collected in a barrel. (Hard tap water is rich in lime; it can be distinguished from soft water by its habit of leaving white deposits in a tea kettle and by lathering soap less well.) Or use distilled water. Never use water softeners in water given to houseplants.

As a rule, water should be lukewarm or at least at room temperature. Cold water will impede plant growth, and stray drops may spot the leaves.

Amount of water Plants vary in their need for water. Some should be watered plentifully, some moderately, and others sparingly.

Generally, plants in active growth, and especially those with delicate leaves, require continuously moist soil. Thick-leaved and succulent foliage plants and cacti store water in their tissues and easily tolerate periods of dryness; they need only moderate amounts of water. During the midwinter months, when plant growth slows down (especially in the North), water should be given sparingly. This also applies to plants kept in a cool room, where transpiration (loss of water from the leaf surfaces) is much less than in a warm atmosphere.

Give enough water at each irrigation so that some will flow out through the drainage holes in the bottom of the pot. Except in rare cases — as with bog and water plants, for instance — do not let the pot stand in excess water. Remember that even the thirstiest plants will suffer if given too much water.

When to water The most obvious sign that a plant requires water is drooping or wilting leaves,

◀ **Misting** Regular sprays with fine, tepid mist keep plant foliage free of dust. Misting also helps to increase the immediate air humidity, but cannot replace routine watering. Never spray plants that have hairy or felted leaves or opening flower buds.

but this is not the most useful indication, since it may come too late. Although thin leaves that have wilted can usually be revived quickly, thicker ones often will not respond. In any case, repeated periods of wilting and resuscitation inhibit plant growth and flower formation and cause leaves to turn brown and then fall off. Wilting can also result from overzealous watering — roots can be damaged or even destroyed by waterlogging.

Testing the potting mix is the only really sure guide to a plant's water requirements, but don't take too much notice of superficial evidence — a dry surface can hide a lot of underlying moisture. Probe for moisture below the soil surface with your finger, a pencil, or a thin wooden stake. Moist soil will stick to the probe.

If still in doubt, lift the pot up and test its weight in your hands. Dry soil weighs much less than moist, and with a little practice you should be able to determine the water content with some accuracy. A clue, when growing plants in clay pots, is the difference in sound when a potful of dry soil or a potful of moist soil is tapped with a hard object. The moist pot will make a much duller sound.

You can buy small moisture-indicator sticks. These are simply pushed into the soil as a permanent feature and display the moisture level by changing color. For the serious indoor gardener, there is also a moisture meter for measuring the moisture content of the potting soil on a very precise scale. This is rather elaborate for ordinary home use but is useful for checking large tubs and containers. It has a long probe, which can be pushed deep into the root system.

Watering methods Woody and long-stemmed plants may be watered from the top of the pot, but rosette-type plants whose leaves grow straight from a low rootstock or corm — such as African violets (Saintpaulia) and cyclamens — should not be watered constantly from the top, as this may cause the crown to rot. Pour

the water into the saucer on which the pot stands and allow the soil to draw it up. Such bottom-watered plants must be occasionally watered thoroughly from the top, too, so that excess salts may be washed down and out of the potting mix.

When you are watering hairy-leaved plants, such as gloxinias (Sinningia) and African violets, avoid spilling drops of water on the foliage, since these drops may discolor and rot the leaves.

How to water To water plants from the bottom, continue filling the saucer until the soil can absorb no more and the surface feels moist to the touch. Then wait half an hour and pour out any water that remains in the saucer.

The beginner's impulse may be to match the amount of water to the plant's need — splashing just a little water on the soil around the base of a cactus and pouring a generous dollop into the pot of some tropical foliage plant such as a philodendron. In fact, it is far

easier and far healthier for the plant to have a potting mix with a moisture-holding capacity that is best for the type of plant you have.

A mixture of 1 part sphagnum peat, 1 part coarse sand, and 1 part loam or perlite is a good formula for most houseplants. For plants that prefer drier soil, such as cacti or succulents, blend this basic mix with an additional part of coarse sand or perlite; for moisture lovers, blend the basic mix with an additional part of coarse sphagnum peat or compost. Having adjusted the potting mix, you can water in the standard manner, relying on the soil to absorb and retain the right amount of moisture for that particular plant.

Commercial potting soils are usually something of an unknown quantity — few list the ingredients and their relative proportions on the bag. When using these soils, indoor gardeners must use their judgment, adding amounts of perlite, leaf mold,

▶ **Dainty fern** A Southern maidenhair fern (Adiantum capillus-veneris) needs filtered light and good humidity. Set the pot on a tray of moist pebbles.

KEEPING LEAVES CLEAN

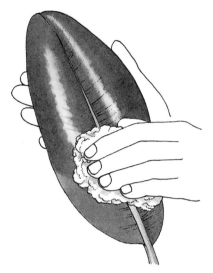

1 From time to time, gently wipe both sides of large-leaved plants with a damp pad of absorbent cotton or facial tissues to clean dust thoroughly from their pores. Use soft rainwater or distilled or boiled water if the tap water is hard. You can mix a little milk with the water to give a glossy sheen.

2 Alternatively, set your plant in the kitchen sink and give it a thorough shower with the spray attachment. This treatment should not be applied to plants with hairy or nappy leaves, since the water will linger, promoting fungal and bacterial infections. Instead, remove dust and dirt with a soft brush (page 19).

sand, or sphagnum peat until the soil looks and feels suitable for the plants at hand. Another difficulty with commercial potting soils is that some are rich in nutrients and others have practically none — and there is no way to tell which is which.

By contrast, peat-based or so-called soilless mixes tend to be precisely formulated and often list ingredients and relative proportions on the bag. Improving such mixtures is therefore a simple and exact process. Peat-based mixes are naturally sterile and devoid of nutrients; if any fertilizer has been added, that will be noted on the bag.

Feeding

Three chemical elements are essential for the balanced growth of all plants: nitrogen, phosphorus, and potassium. Nitrogen, in the form of nitrates, is vital for encouraging stem and leaf growth. Phosphorus, as phosphoric acid or phosphate, promotes healthy root formation. Potassium, as potash, is required for the production of flowers and fruit as well as general plant sturdiness. Every plant also needs minute quantities of a number of other minerals, or trace elements.

Plant foods sold specifically for houseplants have a balanced content and may be formulated for flowering plants, foliage plants, or both types. Those for foliage plants have a relatively high nitrogen content. They may be used for flowering plants in their early stages of growth, when leaf and stem growth is required in preference to flowers.

There are also soluble foliar fertilizers for spraying on foliage. These have an immediate restorative effect on almost any plant that looks starved. Foliar feeding is useful for plants that absorb little food through their roots — bromeliads, for instance. Take plants outside to spray, or put them in the bathtub, since the chemicals stain fabrics.

Houseplant fertilizers come in several forms — liquids, solid "spikes," slow-release capsules or granules, and soluble powders or crystals. Liquids and soluble powders must be diluted in water and applied just after watering. Follow the manufacturer's instructions on the product label for dilution rates.

Spikes are easy to use; push them into the soil according to the maker's instructions. Most modern solid fertilizers release food chemicals gradually without scorching nearby roots.

Applying fertilizers Newly bought or repotted plants should not require immediate feeding. A plant in a soil-based potting mix may not need to be fed for up to 3 months, since the soil contains its own minerals apart from those in any added fertilizer. The fertilizer in peat-based potting mixes, however, is generally used up in 6 to 8 weeks, so feeding should begin within 2 months for newly bought plants or those repotted in such mixtures.

Feed plants only when they are in active growth. If fertilizer is given to a plant during a period of semidormancy or rest, it may result in spindly growth with abnormally small, pale, fragile leaves. Don't give fertilizer to a plant just because it seems sickly — fertilizer is food, not a medicine for plants. Instead, consider whether the trouble may be due to other factors, such as overwatering, drafts, or the wrong air temperature.

FEEDING HOUSEPLANTS

1 Spikes of solid plant food are an easy means of feeding houseplants. Push one spike into each pot. Nutrients will be released continuously over a period of several weeks. Slow-release granules are also available, which should be incorporated into the potting soil.

2 Liquid fertilizer should be applied directly to the soil surface during the active growing season after the plants have been watered — never to dry soil, as the fertilizer will scorch a plant's roots. Follow the maker's instructions precisely for rate of application and dilution.

REVIVING HOUSEPLANTS

Neglect is as great an enemy as pests or diseases, but in most cases proper care and treatment can restore ailing plants to health and vigor.

Some houseplants are more easygoing than others, but all types will become straggly, limp, discolored, and eventually die if they are not treated properly.

The most common form of neglect is due to a long vacation or an unplanned absence from home. Though measures can be taken to give houseplants a slow-release supply of water and nutrients while you are away, the reservoir may dry up before you return.

Sick and neglected plants can usually be brought back to health, provided they are not completely dead. However, the procedure may have to be drastic, so be prepared for some failures.

Among the common causes of a plant's poor health are lack of water and humidity, lack of soil nutrients, lack of space and air, insufficient sunlight, inappropriate room temperatures, and cold drafts. Many of these problems can be corrected immediately, but damaged plants may take weeks or months to recover fully. Watering a wilted plant, however, may give an almost instant response.

Emergency watering

If a plant's leaves or stems are limp and withered and the soil is bone-dry, water must be given right away.

However, if the soil has shrunk away from the sides of the container, watering from the top is useless — the water simply flows down the sides of the root ball and out through the container's drainage holes without wetting the roots. This sort of problem is common with peat-based potting mixes, which dry out and shrink quickly. Once it is dry, peat is very difficult to remoisten.

The best way to saturate dry soil is to submerge the entire pot and root ball in a bucket or bowl of fresh water, so that the water comes right over the top of the pot. If you use a lightweight peat-based mix in a lightweight plastic pot, you may have to hold the pot down to stop it from floating.

Keep the pot submerged until air bubbles cease to rise from the soil. This may take 15 minutes or more if the soil is really dry and compacted. Then lift the pot out

of the water (it will be much heavier now) and allow it to drain thoroughly in the kitchen sink or in the garden if the weather is calm and mild. Finally, return the plant to its place in the home, standing it in a drip saucer.

An additional kind of first aid to administer after rewetting the soil is to cover the plant with a clear plastic bag for a day or two, while keeping it out of direct sunlight. The bag will boost the humidity around the plant's stems and leaves and help them regain their natural turgor.

Do not feed a limp plant until it has fully recovered from lack of water, as dry roots are easily scorched by fertilizers.

If lack of water is the only problem, the plant should recover within a few hours, and certainly within a day or two. Any small leaves that don't stand up again should be cut off; otherwise they may rot.

Overwatered plants

It is just as easy to harm a plant by overwatering as by underwatering. In fact, more houseplants are killed by overwatering than by any other cause. If the foliage is wilting but the soil is wet instead of bone-dry, overwatering is probably to blame. Other symptoms are yellowing leaves, bud drop, premature flower drop, and rotting stems and leaves. If slimy green algae appear on a clay pot, it is a sure sign of overwatering.

Overwatering is a common problem in winter. Many plants go into a period of partial dormancy and need little water, but in trying to be kind to the plants, many people water as frequently and as generously as they did in the summer.

Unlike underwatering, the effects of overwatering can be quite

◄ **Speedy revival** Dried-out soil, high temperatures, and hot sun from a southern window can quickly lead to collapse. Immersion in a tepid bath usually revives a plant.

WATERING DRIED-OUT HOUSEPLANTS

1 Before watering, break up the surface of the soil if it has become encrusted with lime from hard tap water. Loosen the top ½ in (12 mm), so that it will soak up water more readily.

2 Submerge the entire pot in a bowl of tepid water so that the water comes right over the rim. Don't remove the plant until air bubbles stop rising from the surface of the soil.

3 Move the saturated plant to the kitchen sink or stand it outdoors to let excess water drain from the soil before you return the plant to its original site.

difficult to correct — in bad instances, the roots will have partially or completely rotted.

Move an affected plant to a warmer spot, and don't water it again until the soil has dried out. Even then, let the plant stand dry for another week. Drying out may take several weeks in winter because the combination of damaged roots and partial dormancy means that little water is being taken up by the plant.

In summer, drying out may be much quicker. To prevent more damage due to dry air while the plant is recovering, mist the foliage frequently with tepid water; this won't affect soil moisture.

Before resuming normal watering, knock the plant out of its pot and check the roots. If new, whitish, fleshy roots are discernible, the plant should recover without further treatment. However, if only black or brown shriveled roots are visible, tease away most of the soil, cut off the most badly affected roots, and repot the plant in fresh potting mix.

Cleaning dirty leaves
When leaves are dusty, their pores become clogged, preventing air from reaching the respiratory tissues within. Dust also blocks light — another vital component for plant growth and health — from the leaf, as well as ruining the appearance of the plant.
Washing with water To clean dust and dirt from a relatively small, smooth-leaved houseplant, which can be picked up and moved easily, put the plant in the

bathtub or kitchen sink and spray it with water at room temperature. Don't use cold water, as this can damage delicate foliage.

An even easier way is to cup the top of the pot with the palm of your hand to contain the soil and invert the whole plant, dipping the leaves and stems in a large bowl of water. Use slightly soapy water if the leaves are very dirty, but be sure to rinse the leaves in clear water afterward. Never use detergents.

With smooth-leaved plants that are too big to move, as well as those with large leaves, you can wash each leaf individually. Use a sponge or soft cloth moistened with water. Again, if the dust is thick and won't wash off readily, use soapy water followed by a clear-water rinse.

When washing a single leaf, support the leaf blade with one hand and gently sponge or wipe the upper surface with the other hand. Don't try to clean new leaves in this way, since they are too soft and bruise easily. As a general rule, the undersides of leaves need much less attention.

After washing a plant, do not let water remain on the leaves or in the angles between stems and leafstalks — lingering moisture can scorch the leaves of plants that are standing in full sun and rot those in shade.
Brushing Hairy leaves, scaly leaves, and those with a waxy or powdery bloom present special cleaning problems, which are not always easy to solve. Hairy leaves cannot be washed individually,

for instance. Some plants can be sprayed lightly, as long as persistent drops of water are shaken off afterward, but others — such as African violets — hate having their leaves moistened.

Clean hairy leaves with a small, soft brush. The type of brush used for cleaning camera lenses is ideal for this job, or a small, soft-bristled artist's brush may be used.

However, never use even the softest of brushes or cloths for scaly, waxy, or powder-coated leaves. A gentle spraying with some cautious shaking to dry off the moisture is as much as these easily damaged surfaces can bear.

Damaged leaves
In addition to yellowing and general discoloration due to nutrient starvation or incorrect watering, the leaves of neglected plants are often physically damaged by passersby or scorched by too much sunlight. These situations produce bent or broken leaves or leaves with unsightly brown tips or patches.

Brown patches or tips indicate dead tissues that will never recover. The only solution is to cut off the damaged parts. Cut off the whole leaf if the damage is in the middle. But if only the edge or tip is brown, trim these sections off with a sharp pair of scissors, leaving as much healthy green tissue as possible.

In the long term, trimmed leaves may die back farther and need repeated treatment, but substantial defoliation caused by

SIX WAYS TO REJUVENATE HOUSEPLANTS

1 Trim off all dead stems, branches, and individual leaves. Such dead tissue is easy prey for fungi, which once established on the plant may spread to adjacent areas. Also remove any dead leaves as well as other debris that has fallen on the soil at the base of the plant.

2 Dead patches at the tips and edges of leaves look unsightly, but removing each affected leaf could seriously reduce the plant's vigor. Instead, trim off just the brown areas. If leaves die back farther, cut off whole leaves one at a time over several weeks; removing many at once could traumatize the plant.

3 Support floppy stems with thin houseplant stakes. Use slender stakes and insert them toward the outside of the pot to minimize any damage to the roots. Use soft twine to tie in the stems, knotting it to the stake, then looping it around the stem, and finally knotting it behind the stake (inset).

4 Clean dust-laden leaves to allow the pores to breathe freely and to let essential light energy reach the food-producing tissues. Dust delicate hairy or felted leaves with a soft brush, and use a small sponge or soft cloth moistened with tepid water to wipe the upper surfaces of large shiny leaves.

5 Spray pest- or disease-infected plants with an insecticidal soap or a liquid plant insecticide or fungicide. If you do not wish to spray inside the home, invert the container and immerse the top growth for a few seconds in a bowl of soapy water or spray-strength liquid pesticide.

6 Revive a wilted plant by watering it well and then covering the foliage with a clear plastic bag propped up on sticks or a wire hoop. Be sure that the plastic does not touch the leaves. Set the plant in a shaded spot for a couple of days before removing the bag and returning the plant to its window sill.

---

cutting off several whole leaves, just for the sake of eliminating a few brown patches, could seriously weaken the plant. However, if a cut leaf "bleeds" a lot of sap or white latex, it may be better to cut it off at the stalk, where only a small cut surface will remain.

Sometimes it is possible to splint a bent leaf, and in time the tissues will harden across the damaged area. Try this with spider plants *(Chlorophytum)*, for example, which look unsightly if any of their gently arching leaves are creased.

Make a tiny collarlike splint by rolling a length of adhesive tape into a cylinder with the sticky side outward. Feed the collar over the tip of the bent leaf, and position it so that the leaf is bent back to its normal contour. Experiment until the collar is the right size, since if it is too tight the leaf will be bruised.

Carefully slip off the splint after a week or two during active growth, or after about a month if the plant is currently in a resting phase.

Dead stems and branches
Many unsightly houseplants can be transformed by simply pruning away dead or dying stems and branches. Though the remaining stems may be rather widely spaced, the plant should soon flourish, provided it is watered, fed, and given adequate light.

Using sharp pruning shears, scissors, or a pruning knife, cut back dead stems and branches to a point at least ½ in (12 mm) below the base of the dead material, leaving a clean cut through completely healthy tissue. Cut just above a leaf or bud, or just above a collarlike node if no buds are visible. Cut to an outward-facing bud so that the plant can develop a uniform shape.

Lanky growth
A plant that has never been pruned, or has received insufficient light, is often tall and straggly, with long sections of thin stem between each leaf. In severe

cases, the base of the plant may have no leaves at all.

Cutting the plant back ruthlessly may force out new growth from the plant's base. Using pruning shears or a sharp knife, cut the stem close to the base. Doing this should encourage new shoots to form. If the plant is now grown in more suitable conditions and given adequate food and water, the new shoots should be compact and healthy.

If the trimmed-off top growth is not too weak, it can often be salvaged for cuttings. In this way, if the remaining stumps don't

◀ **Leggy begonia** A new lease on life can be given to an overgrown begonia that has lost most of its lower leaves. Cut the stems down to near the base; use the leaves as propagation material. Then knock the root ball out of its pot and repot in fresh soil. New shoots should soon sprout from the base.

produce a satisfactory new plant, the cuttings can provide new stock instead.

Floppy stems

Climbing and scrambling houseplants, such as the popular grape ivy, may be self-supporting when they are young, but as the stems lengthen they fall over, unless a means of support is supplied. Though floppy growth may be perfectly healthy, the overall effect is unattractive.

Even bushy plants, such as impatiens, can flop over with age, especially if they are grown in poor light, where the growth becomes elongated. Straightening the plants will improve their appearance immediately.

Thin canes or stakes are ideal for supporting single stems. Use small metal ring ties or soft twine to tie them in place. For multi-stemmed plants, tie thin bamboo canes together to make an indoor trellis. Don't worry if the undersides of some of the leaves face downward or upward after the stems have been tied in — they will soon twist around to face the light.

Pests and diseases

Many different pests and diseases can attack houseplants, and the symptoms of damage are wide-ranging. Once weakened, leaves, stems, and flowers often succumb to secondary disorders.

It is important to eradicate pests and diseases as soon as you spot them. Better still, carry out routine troubleshooting inspections. Insecticidal soap will probably be a sufficient remedy if the pests are spotted while still few in number, but if a plant has been neglected and the pest has overwhelmed the leaves and stems, a more radical approach may be necessary. This is often the case with red spider mites and whiteflies. These small pests hide on the undersides of a plant's leaves, and they can remain undetected until they reach plague proportions. Put the affected plant in quarantine before it can infect your other plants.

Where possible, cut off and destroy just the affected plant material; otherwise, cut down and destroy almost the entire top growth. If the roots are not affected, the remaining stumps should regrow healthy shoots.

A STRAGGLY PELARGONIUM

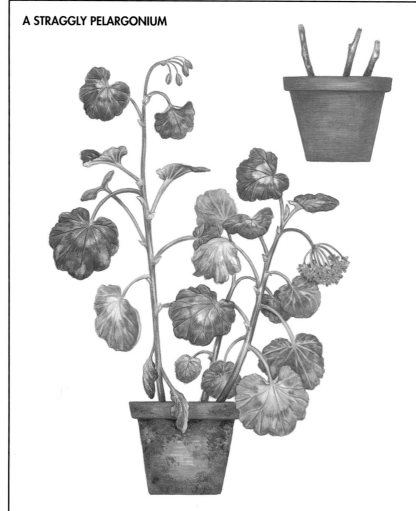

A victim of insufficient light and nutrient starvation, this zonal pelargonium shows signs of deterioration — yellowing and brown leaves; long, thin stems; and poor flowers. New growth can be encouraged by cutting the stems down to a few inches above the soil's surface and repotting. This half-wilted top growth is unsuitable for cuttings.

PROPAGATING HOUSEPLANTS

It is easy, inexpensive, and satisfying to multiply houseplants by various means of propagation, whether from seeds, cuttings, plantlets, division, or air layering.

There are a number of reasons for propagating houseplants: to grow something new that has caught your eye in someone else's home; to grow additional plants of your own stock, perhaps as gifts for friends; or to revitalize old, untidy plants. In any event, the propagation process itself can be so fascinating that many indoor gardeners increase houseplants for their own pleasure.

Two types of propagation are possible. The first — commonly known as vegetative propagation — involves using part of an existing plant, such as an offset, stem, or leaf, or it may simply involve the division of a clump. Although in some cases this method is a natural way by which plants increase themselves, most vegetative propagation methods have been devised by humans.

Nature's usual method of increasing plants is by means of the seeds that result from the reproductive process of flower pollination. Most houseplants can be propagated successfully by this second method. Indeed, there is no other way to increase annual plants grown for their one short season of flowers. In addition, raising perennial houseplants from seed can be an engrossing and inexpensive source of pleasure and pride.

However, because it is often difficult to obtain viable seed — especially from species that rarely or never flower indoors — and because it is sometimes difficult to make seeds germinate successfully, the vegetative methods are much more common among amateur growers of houseplants. What's more, vegetative methods are usually much faster than the process of bringing a seedling to maturity.

The use of indoor propagating units or mist benches in a greenhouse can improve the success rate with certain species, but little equipment is needed for propagating most houseplants. All that is usually needed is some sterilized seed-starting mix or rooting medium. Never use garden soil, as it is likely to contain pests, diseases, and weed seeds and won't provide suitable drainage in a pot. Small, clean food containers, like those for yogurt, are ideal for raising cuttings or seedlings cheaply; just punch drainage holes in the bottom.

The vegetative method of propagating plants may be further divided into two broad categories: those that use only a small, expendable part of the parent plant — such as a leaf, shoot tip, or plantlet — and those that largely destroy the parent. The first is most appropriate when you are taking material from a plant that is in good health.

Destructive methods — division, air layering, and stem cuttings from single-stem plants for example — are recommended only when the parent plant has completely outgrown its allotted space indoors or reached the end of its life.

▶ **Pelargonium cuttings** Pelargoniums make fine houseplants but tend to grow leggy with age. Tip cuttings of young shoots taken at the end of summer will root after 2 or 3 weeks. If exposed to too much moisture in the soil or air, however, the cutting may turn black at the base and collapse.

TAKING SOFT-TIP CUTTINGS

1 Several cuttings can be taken from the stems of a wandering Jew throughout summer. Cut 3 in (7.5 cm) long cuttings from the tips of side shoots, and remove the lower leaves.

2 Trim cuttings cleanly just below a leaf node. Make planting holes around the edge of a 4 in (10 cm) pot. Insert the bottom third to half of the cuttings in the holes, and firm down the rooting medium.

3 Cover the pot with a clear plastic bag held in place with a rubber band. Keep it in a shaded place indoors until the cuttings have rooted — indicated by the appearance of fresh growth.

4 Carefully separate the rooted cuttings. Pot the new plants singly into 4 in (10 cm) pots of potting soil. Water, and keep the pots in a shaded place for a few more weeks.

TAKING LEAFSTALK CUTTINGS

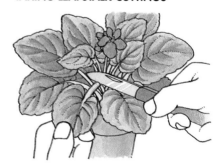

1 Cut healthy young leaves from hairy- or fleshy-leaved species, such as African violets, in summer or early fall. Trim the stalks cleanly.

2 With a small stick, make a few planting holes in a pot of rooting medium. Insert each cutting so that the leaf blade is just clear of the medium.

3 Firm the rooting medium with your fingers, but avoid damaging the stalks. Fill the pot to the top with water, and let it drain. Cover with a clear plastic bag.

4 When a tuft of new leaves has grown from the base of each old leafstalk, pot the cuttings individually in a peat- or compost-enriched potting soil.

CUTTINGS

Increasing plants by cuttings is a common method of vegetative propagation used by indoor gardeners. A small section of a plant is removed and treated so that it becomes a new individual.

Shoot-tip cuttings

Cuttings from hollow- or fleshy-stemmed houseplants, such as impatiens (*Impatiens wallerana*) and wandering Jew (*Tradescantia* and *Zebrina* species and cultivars), and from ivies (*Hedera* species and cultivars) root easily in a number of ways.

Take cuttings from the tips of young, nonflowering stems or side shoots between early and late summer. If only flowering shoots are available, trim off all flowers and flower buds. Strip the lower leaves from a 3-4 in (7.5-10 cm) cutting, and trim it cleanly just below a leaf node. The node is frequently marked by a slightly raised ring of tissue, often with a noticeable sheath that forms at the base of the leafstalk. On woody plants, where the ring and sheath may not be visible, the node can usually be identified by a thickening of the stem and the presence of a leaf scar and a bud if the leaf has fallen off.

Place the cutting in a glass of water in a well-lit position, but shaded from direct sunlight. Roots will usually appear in 10 to 14 days, and the cutting can then be potted.

Most houseplants, especially those with woody stems like dracaenas or poinsettias, will not root in water. Instead, insert their cuttings at once in a rooting medium. Any ready-made seed-starting or potting mixture is suitable, or make your own mixture using equal parts by volume of sphagnum peat and coarse sand or perlite. Fill a 4 in (10 cm) pot with the mixture to just below the rim.

Using a sharp knife, cut off the top 3-4 in (7.5-10 cm) of a non-flowering stem or side shoot. Cut off the lower leaves, and make a clean cut across the stem, just below a leaf node. The best tip cuttings come from sturdy plants with stems whose nodes are relatively close together.

For certain woody-stemmed plants, such as African hemp (*Sparmannia*), a heel cutting is recommended. This is a side shoot pulled off the main stem with a downward tug in such a way as to take with it a heel or small piece of the stem's bark.

Before inserting cuttings into containers of rooting mixture, it is sometimes helpful to dip the cut ends into a hormone rooting powder to stimulate root production. With or without the powder, it is best not to push the prepared cuttings directly into the rooting mixture, unless this is very soft. To avoid injuring cuttings, use small planting holes as follows.

Use a small dibble or stick to make a number of holes 1-1½ in (2.5-3.5 cm) deep in the rooting medium — a 4 in (10 cm) pot will accommodate four to six cuttings. Then, insert the cuttings into the holes and gently firm the rooting medium in around their bases. Finally, fill the pot (or other small container) to the rim with water and leave it to drain.

Cover the pot loosely with a clear plastic bag, and secure it with a rubber band or length of string. Set the pot in a lightly shaded spot, where a temperature of about 65°F (18°C) can be maintained. Alternatively, place the pot in a heated propagating unit. Lift up the cover occasionally to check the moisture content of the rooting medium — it should be damp but not wet. At the same time, discard any cutting that shows signs of rotting.

After 3 or 4 weeks the cuttings should have rooted and the tips will be showing fresh growth. Remove the plastic bag and invert the pot. Separate the rooted cuttings carefully, and pot them individually into 3-3½ in (7.5-9 cm) containers of potting soil.

Water the new young plants carefully, and keep them in a lightly shaded, draft-free place until they are growing well. Once established, move them to their permanent positions.

Leaf cuttings

Houseplants with thick, hairy, or fleshy leaves — African violets *(Saintpaulia)*, begonias, gloxinias *(Sinningia),* and peperomias — are best increased by leaf cuttings. The ideal time for this type of propagation is between early summer and early fall.

Cut healthy leaves, each with a 1-1½ in (2.5-3.5 cm) stalk, from the parent plant. Take only a few leaves at one time; otherwise the parent will be seriously depleted of strength.

Almost fill a 4 in (10 cm) pot with potting soil or rooting medium. Make a few planting holes, slightly less deep than the leafstalks. Trim the end of each leaf

ROOTING CUTTINGS IN WATER

African violets and other soft-stemmed plants can be rooted in water alone. Tie plastic wrap across the top of a water-filled jar. Insert a leafstalk or stem through a hole punched in the plastic. When roots and plantlets form under water, cuttings can be potted up.

stem cleanly across with a sharp knife. Insert the leafstalks into the holes. The base of each stalk should just touch the bottom of the hole, but the leaf blade itself must be clear of the soil, or rot may set in.

Gently pack in the soil around the cuttings with your fingertips, taking extra care not to bruise the fragile stalks, and water them in. Ideally, the cuttings should be left to root in a propagating unit with additional heat, but a suitably warm, humid atmosphere can be produced by enclosing the pot in a plastic bag. If a lot of condensation forms on the inside, it can rot the cuttings — remove the bag and turn it inside out.

After 3 to 5 weeks roots should have formed and new leaves will appear from the base of the leafstalks. Invert the pot and separate the rooted cuttings carefully, without breaking the fine roots. Pot up the cuttings individually in 2½ in (6 cm) pots, and keep the young plants in a warm, lightly shaded position for 2 to 3 weeks until they are established.

Leaf sections

The snake plant *(Sansevieria)* is propagated by a special type of

TAKING LEAF-SECTION CUTTINGS

1 *Sansevieria* is propagated by leaf sections. Cut a leaf away from the crown of the parent plant.

2 Using a sharp knife, cut the leaf cleanly into several 2 in (5 cm) deep horizontal segments.

3 Insert the segments, lower edge down, in a shallow pot of moist potting soil. Cover with a plastic bag.

4 After about 6 weeks the leaf segments will develop into young plants, which can be potted up individually.

LARGE-LEAF CUTTINGS

1 Increase *Begonia rex* and other large-leaved begonias from leaf cuttings. Cut off a healthy leaf, and trim to within ½-1 in (1.2-2.5 cm) of the leaf base.

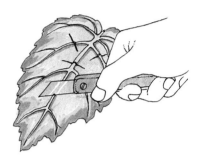

2 Using a sharp knife, make short cuts on the underside of the leaf where the main veins meet. Lay the leaf, cut side down, on moist potting mix in a pot or tray.

3 Weigh the leaf down by placing a few pebbles around the edge. Alternatively, insert pieces of bent wire or hairpins through the leaf blade into the potting mixture.

4 Cover the container with a clear plastic bag, and maintain a temperature of about 70°F (21°C). After a few weeks, small rooted plantlets will appear from the cut vein intersections.

leaf cutting — the straplike, fleshy leaves are cut into horizontal sections, each of which will produce a new plant.

During spring or summer, select a young leaf (preferably a year old) and cut it away close to the plant's crown. Fill a 5 in (13 cm) pot with moist potting soil. Using a sharp knife, cut the leaf horizontally into 2 in (5 cm) segments. Remember which is the top and the bottom of each cutting, as they must be inserted the right way up — any that are inserted upside down won't root. When preparing many leaf segments at once, it is advisable to mark the top edge of each with a small V-shaped nick.

Insert three or four segments, lower side down, in the potting mix to about a third of their depth. Spray the cuttings with tepid water, then place a clear plastic bag over the pot. Keep the cuttings in a shaded position at 70°F (21°C).

When each segment begins to produce a new leaf — often after a considerable time — remove the bag and pot the young plants singly in 3 in (7.5 cm) pots of potting soil. Yellow-edged cultivars of sansevierias do not produce variegated offspring and must be increased by division.

Large-leaf cuttings
Several new plants can sometimes be grown from just one leaf — if it is large enough — as in the case of *Begonia rex* and its many cultivars with colored leaves.

At any time between early summer and early fall, detach a mature leaf and trim the stalk to within ½-1 in (1.2-2.5 cm) of the base. With a sharp knife, make several cuts on the underside where the main veins intersect. Place the leaf, cut side down, on a seed tray or broad pot filled with moist potting mix. Secure the leaf to the potting mix by weighting it with small pebbles, or push wire loops through the leaf.

Cover the tray with a clear plastic bag, and leave it in a lightly shaded spot with a constant temperature of about 70°F (21°C). After about 4 weeks, small plantlets will appear from the cuts. Remove the plastic bag and leave the container in a warm, shady place for 2 to 3 weeks. Then plant up the rooted plantlets individually in small (2½ in/6 cm) pots of potting soil. Keep them lightly shaded and maintain a steady, warm temperature.

OTHER WAYS
Besides the various types of cuttings, several other methods of vegetative propagation are suitable for houseplants. Some of these leave the parent plant more or less intact, but others involve splitting up the parent plant or mutilating it entirely.

Using plantlets
A few houseplant species have a natural ability to increase their numbers by producing miniature

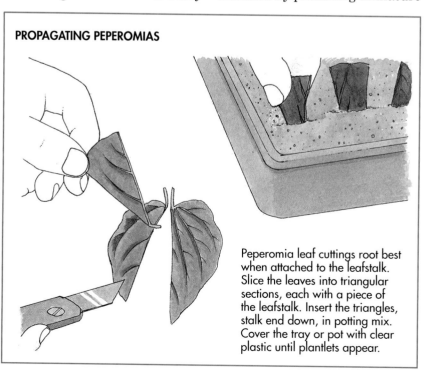

PROPAGATING PEPEROMIAS

Peperomia leaf cuttings root best when attached to the leafstalk. Slice the leaves into triangular sections, each with a piece of the leafstalk. Insert the triangles, stalk end down, in potting mix. Cover the tray or pot with clear plastic until plantlets appear.

replicas of themselves on leaves or stems. These little plants can be detached and grown on.

In some species, plantlets are produced complete with roots, and these develop readily when potted up. More often, however, such plantlets are rootless. In the latter case, the plantlets require careful treatment in order to develop properly after separation from the parent.

On mother-of-thousands detach the threadlike runners, each of which bears a plantlet at its tip, from the parent plant. Nip off the runner from the plantlet.

Almost fill a 2½ in (6 cm) pot with moist potting mix. Make a shallow depression in the surface, and set the plantlet in it. Firm the potting mix around the base of the plantlet. Do not water, but place a clear plastic bag over the pot. Keep out of direct sun and maintain a temperature of 65°-70°F (18°-21°C). The potting mix should be slightly moist at all times.

After about 10 days the plantlet should have rooted. Remove the bag and place the pot in a brighter and cooler place.

Spider plants often bear several plantlets on tough flowering stems. Larger plantlets often develop roots and can be severed from the parent plant and potted up individually. Those that lack roots can be layered into individual 2 in (5 cm) pots of potting mix. To hold the plantlets in place, secure them to the soil with wire hoops. After about 3 weeks the plantlets should have rooted and the stalks can be cut.

Division

Splitting a plant — known as division — is the easiest method of propagation, and new offspring develop quickly. However, only certain types of houseplants can be increased in this way. Each plant must have at least two, and preferably several, stems arising from or below the crown, each with an independent, well-developed root system.

Suitable plants for division are aspidistra, maidenhair fern *(Adiantum)*, fittonia, umbrella sedge *(Cyperus)*, nephrolepis fern, peperomia, spider plant, and snake plant *(Sansevieria)*.

Houseplants can be divided at any time during the growing period — late spring to early fall.

PLANTLETS AND RUNNERS

1 Mother-of-thousands *(Saxifraga stolonifera)* produces threadlike stolons or runners that bear plantlets. These can be pinched off and grown on.

2 Firm each plantlet into a pot of potting mix. Cover with a plastic bag, and keep the pot in a warm, shaded place until roots have formed.

THE RANGE OF NATURAL PLANTLETS

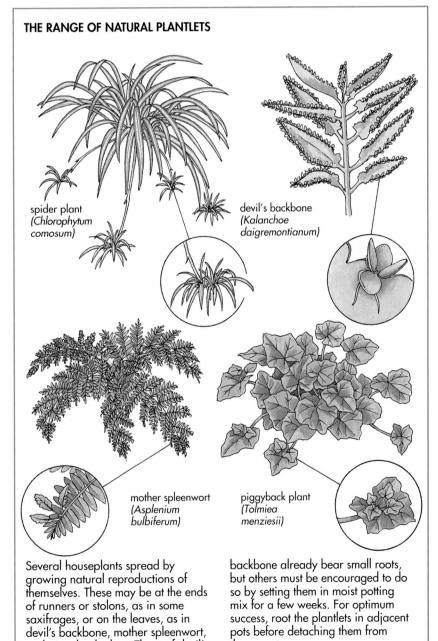

spider plant *(Chlorophytum comosum)*

devil's backbone *(Kalanchoe daigremontianum)*

mother spleenwort *(Asplenium bulbiferum)*

piggyback plant *(Tolmiea menziesii)*

Several houseplants spread by growing natural reproductions of themselves. These may be at the ends of runners or stolons, as in some saxifrages, or on the leaves, as in devil's backbone, mother spleenwort, and piggyback plant. Those of devil's backbone already bear small roots, but others must be encouraged to do so by setting them in moist potting mix for a few weeks. For optimum success, root the plantlets in adjacent pots before detaching them from the parent.

DIVIDING MULTISTEMMED PLANTS

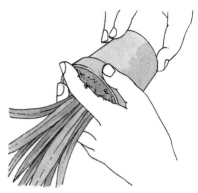

1 Invert the pot and place your fingers around the stems. Knock the rim of the pot against the edge of a table or workbench to dislodge the soil and root ball.

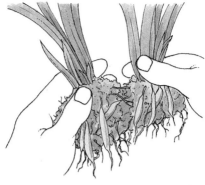

2 Ease away the old, loose soil and carefully pull the crowns and roots of the plant apart. Cut away any damaged or dead roots with a sharp knife or a razor blade.

3 Set each divided piece in a pot partly filled with potting soil. Spread out the roots and trickle in more soil so that the crown will rest just below the rim of the pot.

4 Fill the pot with more soil, and level it about ½ in (12 mm) below the top of the rim. Water sparingly at first, and grow the division on in a warm, lightly shaded location.

the pot with water and allow it to drain.

Tall offsets will need staking for a couple of months, until the root systems are well established and can support the top growth. Insert a thin stake close to the plant, and secure it with wire ring ties or soft twine.

Set the plant in a well-lit spot, but out of direct sun, for a few weeks — a northwest-facing windowsill is the ideal place. Keep the soil moist.

Stem sections
Sections from the lower part of the main stem of certain woody plants can be chopped into pieces and then encouraged to produce roots and shoots. Each piece is trimmed just above a node, and the top section is treated as a tip cutting. Suitable plants include dracaenas (*Dracaena* or *Cordyline* spp.) and dumbcane (*Dieffenbachia*). The Polynesian ti plant (*Cordyline terminalis*) is often given as a gift in the form of short pieces of cane ready to plant.

Stem-section propagation can be adopted when cutting back the stem from which a tip cutting has already been taken — in fact, if

Knock the plant out of its pot, and tease away the soil around the crown and root ball. This will expose the points at which the plant can be divided.

Grasp the base of the plant in both hands, and pull it gently but firmly apart. If the crown or rootstock is thick and tough, sever the largest roots or the underground stems with a sharp knife. Pot the separated pieces at once in potting soil. Water sparingly at first, and keep the pots in a shaded, warm place for a few weeks.

Certain plants — especially the shrimp plant (*Justicia brandegeana*), wandering Jew (*Tradescantia*), and pilea — are often grown commercially from three or more cuttings in the same small pot. As these grow, they form one single mass, which can later be divided by pulling it apart. Pot up the pieces singly.

Separating offsets
Most of the bromeliads — such as *Aechmea, Billbergia,* and *Vriesea*

species — as well as other houseplants, including fatsias, amaryllis (*Hippeastrum*), aglaonemas, and several cacti, readily produce offsets or suckers. These small plants, which appear at the base of the parent, either close to it or a short distance away, may overcrowd the pot as they expand.

Offsets that have reached about a third of the height of the parent plant can be removed easily and potted up separately. The best time for this type of propagation is between early and late summer.

Remove the plant from the pot, and crumble away the excess soil. Hold the root ball, stems upward, in one hand, and tear or cut away the offset, complete with roots — but take care not to break them.

Place a layer of moist potting mix in a 3-4 in (7.5-10 cm) pot, and position the offset on top so that the top of the crown is just below the rim of the pot. Trickle in more potting mix, and firm this with your fingers. Finally, fill

BROMELIAD OFFSETS

Pulling apart the leaves of a blushing bromeliad (*Neoregelia*) reveals an offset suitable for separation. After removing the plant from its pot, sever the offset as close as possible to the main stem, using a sharp knife. Insert the detached offset in a rooting mixture at the same depth as it was growing before.

the plant has grown leggy, it is often necessary to remove such stems to restore it to a more attractive shape. If the stem is a thick one, short pieces may be used. Each stem piece need be no more than 2 in (5 cm) long, provided it has one or two nodes. The position of the cuts in relation to the nodes is unimportant. Nick the base of each stem section to indicate which way it should be potted up.

Insert the short, thick cuttings into the rooting mixture vertically, half-burying them, with a node or leaf bud facing upward and the nicked edge in the rooting mix. Or lay the sections horizontally on the rooting medium and cover the ends lightly until roots develop at one end.

Air layering

Eventually rubber plants *(Ficus elastica)*, false aralias *(Dizygotheca elegantissima)*, and certain other upright plants grow too tall and lose their lower leaves. Rather than throwing the plant away, propagate it by air layering in spring to produce a shorter-stemmed plant.

Using a sharp knife, remove all leaves 6-9 in (15-23 cm) below the growing tip. Cut the leaves flush with the stem, being careful not to wound the stem tissues. Then make a shallow upward-slanting cut about 1½ in (3.5 cm) long, starting below a node. Tie the stem to a stake, above and below the cut. Prop the cut open with a small wedge or matchstick. Brush both sides of the wound with rooting hormone powder.

Wrap a piece of plastic sheet around the cut. The piece should be about 6-7 in (15-18 cm) wide and long enough to come 3-4 in (7.5-10 cm) below and above the cut. Seal with adhesive tape below the cut to create a tube or sleeve. The use of clear plastic makes it easier to see when rooting has taken place, but black plastic excludes sunlight and may encourage better rooting.

Next, fill the plastic sleeve with moist sphagnum moss or moist sphagnum peat, pressing it into and around the cut with a small stick or dibble. Then seal the top of the filled sleeve with tape, so that the rooting medium will remain moist.

After 8 to 10 weeks the open wound should have produced

STEM-SECTION CUTTINGS

1 An overgrown *Dracaena fragrans* that has lost its lower leaves may no longer be attractive. It is an obvious candidate for propagation from thick stem cuttings.

2 Using a sharp knife or pruning shears, cut the main stem into several short pieces, each of which should take root and produce shoots as long as it contains at least one healthy leaf node.

3 Stem sections may be placed in a rooting medium either horizontally or vertically, the same way up as the original plant — stems inserted upside down will not root successfully.

4 Leaf shoots develop from nodes exposed to the air, while roots sprout from buried nodes. When a couple of leaves have unfurled, pot each cutting individually in potting soil.

AIR-LAYERING A RUBBER PLANT

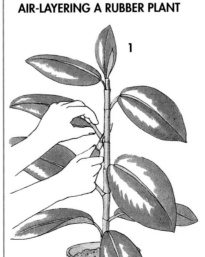 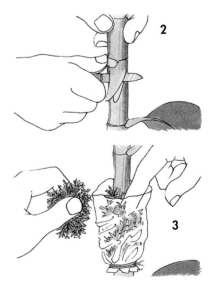

In spring, remove any leaves about 6-9 in (15-23cm) below the top cluster on an overgrown plant (**1**). Cut the leaves flush with the stem. Then make a slanting, upward cut, about 1½ in (3.5 cm) long, from below a

node (**2**). Open out the cut, and brush with rooting powder. Secure a plastic sleeve over the cut, and pack with moist sphagnum moss or peat (**3**). When roots are visible, sever the shoot and pot it up.

PROPAGATION BY SEED

1 Before sowing dustlike seeds in seed-starting mix, sift some of the mixture through a fine strainer. This finely ground top layer will stop the seeds from sinking too deeply.

2 Scatter the seeds thinly. With experience, you can shake them directly from the seed packet. Or mix them with some sand, and sprinkle small pinches between your forefinger and thumb.

3 Water in the seeds with a fine spray from a mister or florist's bulb. Then cover the pot with glass or plastic to maintain humidity. Some surface-sown seeds must be shaded from light.

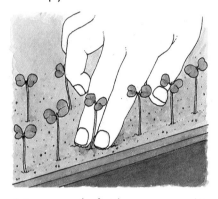

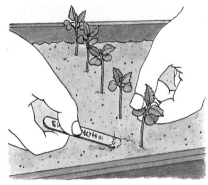

4 As soon as the first leaves appear, thin out the seedlings drastically; they need space for their developing root systems. After thinning, gently firm the seed-starting mix around the seedlings.

5 When each seedling is growing strongly, and before its roots become entangled, ease it out of the seed-starting mix. A plastic plant label makes a useful tool for this purpose.

6 Transplant each seedling singly into a small pot of potting mix. Hold the seedling by a leaf, which is expendable — not by its delicate and irreplaceable stem.

roots. When this has occurred, sever the shoot below the sleeve and carefully free the roots from the plastic and moss. Discard the old plant, or let it grow on to produce side shoots.

Place the new plant in a 4 in (10 cm) pot of potting mix. For the first few weeks — until the new root system is established — grow the plant at 65°-70 °F (18°-21°C) and mist the leaves every day with tepid water.

Seed propagation
Houseplant seed is becoming increasingly available. In addition to the common impatiens, cyclamen, celosia, coleus, cineraria, primula, and streptocarpus, exotic plants such as the bird-of-paradise flower *(Strelitzia)*, banana plants *(Musa)*, as well as angel's trumpet *(Datura)* are being offered. Though it takes longer to develop mature plants from seed than from other forms of propagation, this is the only method of propagating hybrid strains. It is

also a rewarding way of growing many varieties of houseplants.

Seeds come in all sizes, from tiny dustlike specks to large avocado-size pits. Mix the tiniest ones with a little sand in a saucer to make them more visible and hence easier to sow thinly and uniformly.

Sowing time and the required temperature for germination vary — follow the recommendations given on the packet. Most houseplant seeds need a minimum temperature of 65°F (18°C), but some need as much as 80°F (27°C).

Sow seeds thinly in a commercial seed-starting mix. As a rule, it is better to have seeds left over than to sow too many, since well-spaced seedlings will develop a better shape and are less prone to damping-off disease. Large seeds will often benefit from being soaked overnight in water before sowing. Other seeds have tough coats, which should be nicked with a sharp knife to weaken them. Use a slicing action that

barely perforates the seed coating and does not injure the embryo within.

Cover small but visible seeds with a thin sprinkling of finely screened seed-starting mix. Cover larger seeds with a layer equivalent to twice their diameter. Dustlike seeds, however, should not be covered at all — just mist them with water to settle the seeds into the surface of the mix.

Keep the seed-starting mixture moist, but not wet, at all times; tiny seeds in particular will shrivel and die, even after just a few hours of dryness. However, constant watering disturbs seeds, so it is best to maintain a humid atmosphere, thus reducing the need to water them. Place the container in a propagating unit or cover it with a sheet of glass or clear plastic until the young seedlings emerge.

When they are large enough to handle, transplant seedlings into small pots of potting soil and grow them on.

HOUSEPLANTS FOR FREE

Exotic and unusual houseplants can be grown from the pits and seeds that are usually discarded from edible tropical fruits.

Don't throw away the pits and seeds of edible fresh fruits that you buy at the fruit stand or supermarket, especially if they are exotic types. Many are fertile and can be germinated to produce handsome potted plants for the windowsill or greenhouse.

Even if the houseplants you grow are not successful in the long run, the experiment can be both educational and fascinating. Sometimes the most enthusiastic gardeners do not know what the parent plants of many fruits they buy look like. Remember, though, that the pits and seeds found in canned fruits and roasted nuts will never germinate.

Germinating tropical seeds

The following plants are quite easy to grow from seed and will give reliable results. Children especially will enjoy this project, and the final plants will look attractive indoors.

Avocado *(Persea americana,* syn. *P. gratissima)* has one huge pit in the center. When the fruit is ripe and ready to eat, the pit is potentially capable of germination — in fact, when a very ripe avocado is cut open, the pit's mahogany-brown skin is often already split.

Gently wipe away any green flesh from the surface of the pit, then soak it for about 2 days in a bowl of tepid water. Keep the water warm by placing the bowl over a radiator or in a sunny, sheltered spot — cold water can inhibit the germination of this tropical plant.

Don't peel the pit unless the brown skin is flaky. To encourage germination, suspend the pre-soaked pit in the neck of a jar filled almost to the top with water. The simplest way of providing support for the pit is to push the tips of three toothpicks into the sides. This causes no real harm; indeed, the bruising may actually stimulate germination.

The egg-shaped pit must stand fattest end downward; make sure that the base of the pit remains submerged to a depth of ⅜-¾ in (1-2 cm) until a root sprouts from it, which generally takes 5 to 8 weeks, perhaps more in winter. If the water turns cloudy, throw the pit away and start afresh; it has rotted inside.

The first sign of germination is a wormlike white taproot emerging from the base of the pit, even though the pit may have split open beforehand. A few weeks later a shoot will appear at the top of the pit. When this happens, the avocado needs plenty of light, so put it on a sunny windowsill.

The shoot will grow quickly.

◀ **Sweet potato** Related to the morning glory rather than the ordinary potato, sweet potato *(Ipomoea batatas)* is an edible tuber from the tropics. In the wild it grows naturally as a scrambling climber, with lush foliage and scarlet trumpet flowers.

The tubers can be grown indoors for ornamental purposes. Simply wedge them, root end downward, in the neck of a bottle or jar of water; long fibrous roots and clambering shoots will soon develop, though the plant will not bear flowers.

GROWING AN AVOCADO PLANT

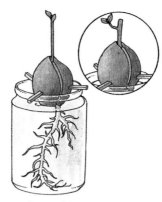

1 Soak a pit for 2 days in tepid water. There is no need to remove the skin unless it peels away easily. Then push the tips of three toothpicks into the sides of the pit, and balance it in the neck of a jar that is filled almost to the top with water.

2 Keep the jar filled with water at all times, with the base of the pit submerged to a depth of ⅜-¾ in (1-2 cm). Roots should appear after 5 to 8 weeks, followed by a slender shoot. When the shoot reaches 6 in (15 cm) in height, snip off the top (inset).

3 A new shoot will soon develop from just below the cut top. This will be less vigorous than the original shoot, making a better-shaped final plant. Carefully pot up the seedling so that the top of the pit stands just above the surface of the potting mix.

4 Avocado plants grow rapidly and will need annual repotting. They tend to produce a tall, bare stem with several large, slender leaves at the top. Pinch off the tip of the main stem when the required height is reached. Support the stem with a stake if necessary.

When it is 6 in (15 cm) tall, cut off the tip, leaving just a bare stalk. Left untrimmed, it grows lanky and fails to develop side shoots. Surprisingly, a new shoot will soon grow from the top of the cut stalk; this shoot grows more slowly and is more compact in habit.

At this stage — or earlier, if you prefer — pot up the young plant, setting the top of the pit just above the surface of moist potting soil. Large evergreen leaves develop, and within 1½ to 2 years it will become a stately houseplant.

Citrus fruits, such as lemons (*Citrus limon*), oranges (*C. sinensis* and *C. aurantium*), tangerines (*C. reticulata*), grapefruits (*C. × paradisi*), and limes (*C. aurantifolia*), typically contain seeds, though some types are seedless.

If the seeds are plump, they can be germinated in pots of seed-starting mix to produce attractive foliage plants with a tangy aroma. Though they are unlikely to yield edible fruits indoors, their white flowers are pretty and powerfully scented.

If you have a garden room or heated greenhouse, citrus plants can be grown on into large shrubs or small trees, which will bear edible fruits.

The best time of year to sow citrus seeds is early spring, but gentle warmth should promote germination at any time of the year. For the best results, use a peat-based seed-starting mix. Since there is no need to store the seeds or treat them in any way, just sow them fresh, placing them on their sides, at a depth equal to twice the seed's diameter. Citrus

seeds sprout within a few weeks.

If you sow a single seed from an orange or lime, you may find that two or three shoots emerge. Only one is a true seedling; the others are a special form of vegetative offspring that develop asexually within the seed shell.

The true seedling has features that are slightly dissimilar to those of the parent and is least likely to bear edible fruits. The vegetative offspring are all identical to the parent and are potential bearers of edible fruit.

Within a few years seedlings develop into bushy plants about 3-4 ft (90-120 cm) tall.

Coffee beans (*Coffea arabica*) can be obtained from some delicatessens and gourmet coffee shops in a fresh, unroasted state. (Roasted coffee beans will not germinate.) Sow the fresh beans in spring in pots of seedling compost. Maintain a temperature of 70°-77°F (21°-25°C) until you see the seedlings emerge.

Coffee plants are bushy with evergreen, glossy dark green leaves. They may eventually produce clusters of attractive white, strongly fragrant flowers followed by green berries, which turn red and then nearly black as the coffee beans ripen within.

However, coffee plants are grown indoors mainly for their foliage value — the beans will be of poor quality.

Date palms (*Phoenix dactylifera*) can be grown from fresh date pits, making elegant plants with a tropical air for the home or greenhouse. The pits are fairly difficult to germinate, but the effort can be worthwhile.

As a tropical plant, the date needs plenty of warmth to start growing. Lightly sandpaper or file the surface of each pit to roughen it; this allows moisture to penetrate more easily.

Next, soak the pits in tepid water for 2 days. Prepare several pits even if you want just one plant, because many are infertile.

Mix the soaked pits with a few handfuls of moist potting soil in a watertight plastic bag. Seal the bag and put it in a warm spot. Check the contents of the bag weekly and remoisten the potting mix if necessary.

When small shoots or roots appear, pot up the seedlings singly with the pit about 1 in (2.5 cm) below the surface. Place the pots

▶ **Peanut plants** These little annuals are fascinating plants for a warm, sunny spot in the home. Their cloverlike growth is not spectacular, but yellow pea flowers produce seedpods that the plants self-sow by bending their stems downward into the ground or potting mix. Peanuts develop and ripen underground within the pod.

in a sunny spot and keep them moist.

Growth is slow, and for several months each seedling will resemble a blade of grass. After 2 or 3 years young plants will have developed a small spray of fanlike leaves, but don't expect flowers or fruits on pot-grown palms.

Keep plants moist during active growth, but let them dry out between waterings in winter. Don't put date palms in too large a pot — they like to have their roots slightly confined.

Peanuts *(Arachis hypogaea)* will germinate, provided they have not been roasted, to produce unusual low-growing or scrambling houseplants.

The peanut plant is an annual, closely related to peas, beans, and clover. In temperate climates, it is grown mainly for its curiosity value. The edible part is a kernel, not a true nut.

Choose nuts sold in the shell. Open the shells carefully and discard (or eat) any nuts that have split in half. Alternatively, leave the peanuts in their husks, but gently split one side to let in moisture. Preshelled unroasted peanuts are also suitable, but again use only whole ones. Keep in mind that the germination of preshelled peanuts is less reliable.

Sow peanuts about 1 in (2.5 cm) deep, three to four in a 5 in (13 cm) pot filled with moist seed-starting mix. The best time of year is spring, but they can be sown at any time of year.

Keep the pot at a minimum temperature of 70°F (21°C), preferably in a heated propagating unit, until seedlings emerge. This usually takes a couple of weeks.

Once the seeds have germinated, move the pot to a warm, sunny windowsill and keep it well watered. Growth resembles that of clover, though peanut plants are more robust.

Yellow pea flowers appear in summer; these are followed by seedpods — the plant's most interesting feature. As they age, the pods bend down and bury themselves in the soil; hence the need for a soft, porous potting mix.

Pineapples *(Ananas comosus)* are bromeliads and can often be grown from the leafy tuft at the top of each fruit. When buying a pineapple, select one that has an unbruised, healthy-looking top. Grayish leaves are normal and not a sign of disease.

Cut off the top with a ½ in (12 mm) thick slice of the juicy flesh attached. Put this aside for a day

GROWING LEMONS FROM SEEDS

1 Fill a 4 in (10 cm) pot with seed-starting mix, water thoroughly, and leave it to drain. Bury four to six fresh lemon seeds about ½ in (12 mm) deep, positioning them on their sides.

2 Cover the pot loosely with a piece of clear plastic, securing it with a rubber band. Keep the pot in a warm place with a minimum temperature of 65°F (18°C) until seedlings emerge.

3 Pot up the seedlings individually as soon as they are large enough to handle. Repot the lemon plants whenever they become pot-bound, using ordinary potting soil.

GROWING A PINEAPPLE

1 Select a pineapple with a healthy tuft of unbruised leaves. It will have the best flavor, and it may be possible to root the top. Cut off the crown below the upper row of scales on the skin.

2 Store the top on its side for 1 or 2 days, until the cut surface of the flesh has dried out. Then plant the pineapple top in a pot filled with an acidic potting mixture.

3 Sprinkle potting mix around the crown of the pineapple so that the fleshy base is just buried; as you do so, beware of the sharp spines on the leaves. Firm in with your fingers and water well.

4 Cover the pot with a clear plastic bag, securing it with a rubber band. Cut off the corners of the bag to allow a little air to circulate inside. Keep the plant warm (minimum 65°F/18°C).

5 Rooting is indicated by new growth from the center of the leaf rosette and by the greening of the existing leaves. At this time remove the bag. Repot the plant into a larger pot as necessary.

---

or two, until the cut surface of the flesh has dried out. Peel away any brown leaves around the base of the tuft.

Plant the pineapple top in a pot filled with a peat-based, lime-free potting mixture. Water the mix, then cover the pot with a clear plastic bag until new leaves appear at the center of the tuft and the existing leaves start to grow larger — a sign that the pineapple top has rooted.

After several years, the plant may flower and produce a small, inedible fruit, but it is for their stiff, spiny leaves that pineapples are valued indoors.

Other plants to try

For further experimentation, try germinating the seeds or pits of kumquats (*Fortunella japonica* and *F. margarita*), loquats (*Eriobotrya japonica*), lychees (*Litchi chinensis*), and pomegranates (*Punica granatum*).

Also try tangelos, jujubes, mangoes, and some of the other unusual fruits that are becoming more and more common on supermarket shelves — they will all prove to be fascinating in their individual ways.

For small quantities of seed, 3-4 in (7.5-10 cm) pots are ideal, but sow larger numbers in a seed tray. As a general rule, sow seeds at a depth equal to twice their diameter in commercial seed-starting mix.

A warm, humid atmosphere is likely to encourage germination of tropical species, so cover the pot or tray with a plastic bag, or place it inside a propagating unit. A temperature of about 65°F (18°C) is suitable for most types of seeds.

When seedlings become large enough to handle, transplant them into individual small pots filled with ordinary loam-based potting mix. Pot on into larger

pots when the root balls become congested and fill the old pots — roots emerging from the drainage hole in the pot's bottom are a clue. The beginning of the spring growing season is a good time to accomplish this.

Large, stony-coated pits may require special treatment before they will germinate. Peach pits, for example, need to be subjected to low temperatures (maximum 39°F/4°C), perhaps in a refrigerator, for several weeks before sowing. (In nature, the fallen fruit has to overwinter before the pits are ready to germinate.)

Climbing plants, such as kiwifruits (*Actinidia chinensis*), grapes (*Vitis vinifera*), melons (*Cucumis melo*), and passion fruits (*Passiflora edulis*), don't make good long-term houseplants, but they can be grown in a greenhouse, either in large pots or in the ground. They must be provided with suitable support.

GROWING INDOOR BULBS

**Pots and bowls of brightly colored and
sweetly scented flowers add a touch of spring
to the indoor garden in midwinter.**

Of the thousands of spring bulbs on sale in late summer and early fall, many have been stored in special conditions so that they can be induced or forced to flower indoors months before they would open in the garden. Hyacinths, narcissi, early tulips, and large-flowered crocuses are popular bulbs for forcing into bloom by Christmas if given special care.

All bulbs and corms contain immature leaf and flower buds, which begin to develop when they are placed in a suitable growing medium — potting soil or plain water. However, in order to produce a fine flowering display, it is essential to establish a strong and healthy root system; to do this, expose the potted bulbs to cool, moist, and dark conditions for a couple of months.

Forcing bulbs

All kinds of containers can be used for indoor bulbs, including flower pots and ceramic, terracotta, and glass bowls (as well as kits complete with a container, a special growing medium, and growing instructions). Ordinary loam-based potting mix works well, though it is best to alter it with bonemeal, adding 1 qt (1 L) of bonemeal per bushel (35 L) of soil.

Moisten the potting mix well before placing it in the container; set the bulbs on top, packing them close together. Small bulbs should ideally end with their tops about 1 in (2.5 cm) below the rim of the container, while the top halves of large bulbs (such as hyacinths and narcissi) can be exposed. Fill in the spaces between the bulbs with more potting mix to hold them steady; leave a space of ½ in (12 mm) below the rim and fill this with water.

Wrap the containers in newspaper and place them in a cool and dark room where temperatures will range from 40°-45°F (4.5°-7°C). In zone 8 and southward, use a refrigerator. Where winters are cold, the pots may be set outdoors. In more temperate regions, such as zone 7, a large

box in which the pots are insulated with 6 in (15 cm) of peat moss may be set in a shaded spot, such as a north-facing wall. Where winters are more severe, the pots should be plunged in gravel, coarse sand, or perlite beneath 6 in (15 cm) of soil covered with black plastic.

Every 2 or 3 weeks, check that the containers have not dried out;

▼ **Spring-flowering bulbs** Dainty narcissi and cheerful crocuses are familiar sights in spring. They are ideal for forcing into early bloom indoors and can be planted out in the garden later on. Tender bulbs — such as lachenalias, with strap-shaped leaves and tricolored flowers, and striking veltheimias, with huge, wavy leaves and 2 ft (60 cm) tall flower stems — need warmer indoor conditions throughout the year as well as an annual rest period.

POTTING BULBS FOR FORCING

1 In early fall, pot up bulbs for forcing, using moistened loam-based potting soil, or vermiculite for containers without drainage holes. Vermiculite encourages roots but contains no nourishment, so bulbs eventually shrivel.

2 Add potting soil or vermiculite so that the tops of small bulbs finish ½ in (12 mm) below the final surface of the soil. The tops of large bulbs can finish above the rim. Fill with more soil or vermiculite, leveling it ½ in (12 mm) below the rim.

3 Moisten vermiculite-filled containers well, but do not soak; fill containers with drainage to the rim with water and leave to drain. Then wrap the containers in newspaper and place them in a cool, dark place. Check occasionally to see that the growing medium stays just moist.

moisten the potting mix if necessary. When the shoots are 1-2 in (2.5-5 cm) tall, move the containers into better light with temperatures of no more than 50°F (10°C). When the shoots have grown about 4 in (10 cm) high, the bowls can be moved to their flowering positions. A cool, well-lit windowsill is the ideal spot.

Remove the flowers as they fade, but leave the stems and foliage intact to nurture the bulbs; move the containers to a cool room and keep them watered until the foliage dies down. Then pop the bulbs out of the containers and plant them in the garden.

Water culture
Hyacinths, early narcissi, and crocuses can also be grown in water. Special hyacinth glasses are available, but any vase or container with a narrow neck in which the bulbs can sit comfortably is suitable. Fill the glass with plain tap water to ½ in (12 mm) above the neck (adding a small lump of charcoal keeps the water clean and sweet-smelling). Place one bulb in each glass so that the bulb base touches the water. Keep the hyacinth glasses in a dark and cool but frost-free place until 4 in (10 cm) long roots and 1 in (2.5 cm) long shoot tips have developed. Move them into better light and warmer conditions for the flowering period.

Crocuses and tazetta narcissi will grow in shallow waterproof containers filled with a good layer of pebbles. Add water to cover the pebbles just to the bulb bases; refill as roots develop and flower stems grow. Nonhardy tazetta-type narcissi bulbs do not need to be kept in the dark and may blossom on a well-lit windowsill in about 6 weeks.

Bulbs grown in water use up all their stored nourishment and are unlikely to ever recover; discard them after flowering.

Untreated bulbs
Most hardy garden bulbs can be brought indoors to flower, but it is the spring-flowering types that generally give the greatest pleasure. Snowdrops and winter aconites, miniature blue and purple *Iris reticulata* and *I. histrioides*, glory of the snow (*Chionodoxa*), grape hyacinths (*Muscari*), scillas, and species crocuses and tulips are all compact enough to

bring color to the indoor garden.

At fall planting time in the North, reserve some bulbs for putting in pots and well-drained bowls of good potting soil. Leave the pots outdoors or in a frost-free garage or cold frame (depending on the severity of the climate) until growth is well advanced; they can then be brought indoors from mid- or late winter onward and will blossom about 3 weeks earlier than in the garden. All do best in a cool and bright site. After flowering, move the pots outdoors again and plant out the bulbs in spring.

The sweetly scented lily of the valley (*Convallaria majalis*), which flowers in late spring, can be forced into bloom in winter. In late fall, before the foliage dies down completely, dig up a clump of the rhizomatous roots, making sure there are plenty of plump buds visible; pot them in potting soil with added sand for drainage. Keep the pots in a cool greenhouse or cold frame for a couple of months, then bring the pots indoors to good light and a temperature of about 68°F (20°C) for flowering in late winter. Keep the potting soil moist at all times.

Tender bulbs
Many exotic bulbous plants are not hardy enough for growing in the garden but make fine indoor flowering potted plants. Blooming at different times of the year, depending on the species, they include hippeastrums, fall- and winter-flowering florist's cyclamens, summer-blooming gloriosa lilies, and dainty Cape cowslips (*Lachenalia*).

Tender bulbs should be grown in loam-based potting mix. Large bulbs, such as clivias and hippeastrums, are spectacular specimen plants, while freesias, Cape cowslips, and star-of-Bethlehem (*Ornithogalum arabicum*) should be planted six or more to a 5 in (13 cm) pot. Place large bulbs so that their tips are level with the surface of the potting mix, 1 in (2.5 cm) below the pot rim; pot small bulbs with tips 1 in (2.5 cm) below the surface.

Most tender bulbs die down after flowering, when the foliage turns yellow; they should then be given a rest period, in cool temperatures and with little or no water, until the growth cycle is restarted with renewed watering.

▲ **Soilless cultivation** Many bulbs, especially hyacinths and bunch-flowered narcissi, flower easily when grown in water only. Special hyacinth glasses are readily available, but any glass container or vase with a constricted neck is suitable. The bulbs must be forced in a dark, cool, frost-free location until roots have developed and the growing shoots are a couple of inches tall.

▶ **Greigii tulips** Notable for their handsome foliage, striped or marbled with purple-maroon, greigii tulips flower in the garden in midspring. Growing no more than 9 in (23 cm) high, the bright scarlet 'Red Riding Hood' can be brought indoors in late winter in order to flower several weeks early. Prechilled bulbs of early single and double tulips can be forced to flower by Christmas.

▶ **Bunch-flowered narcissi** The pure white tazetta narcissi 'Paper White' will flower within 6 weeks of being planted. When grown in potting soil on permanently moist pebbles, each bulb produces several stems, 1 ft (30 cm) high, topped with sweet-scented flowers. Keep them on a well-lit windowsill where the temperature is not too high. The bulbs are tender but suitable for garden planting in the South.

▼ **Basket plantings** Winter resembles early spring with a colorful indoor display of polyanthus primroses, blue and pinkish red hyacinths, and elegant *Cyclamen persicum*. After blooming, primroses and hyacinths can be planted out in the garden for flowering the following year. After a dry summer rest, the cyclamen is easily induced to flower indoors year after year.

HOUSEPLANT PROBLEMS

**Most difficulties associated with houseplants can
be avoided by maintaining a program of routine care.
But a few pests and diseases need special attention.**

Indoor plants are isolated from nature and from the pests and diseases that lurk in the wild, especially the soilborne types. So if you make sure that the plants you bring into your home are pest free, your pest and disease problems will be minimal.

Keep in mind, though, that cut flowers and plants in a window box or outdoors near a window can be way stations for pests moving from the outside in, especially mobile pests such as whiteflies, caterpillars, aphids, and spider mites. Diseases that are airborne invade more readily. In all cases, the best way to keep houseplants healthy is to give them ideal growing conditions.

When you buy a houseplant or transfer one from a greenhouse to the home, give it a few weeks of quarantine in a room without other plants, to make sure that the new plant isn't bringing pests or diseases that will spread to the rest of your houseplants. Watch for signs of trouble, and take immediate action if pests or diseases are spotted. They can strike at any time of year indoors.

Potted plants that have been growing in a greenhouse or have spent the summer in the garden may harbor troublesome garden pests, such as snails, slugs, and caterpillars. Examine the plants thoroughly, checking both sides of the leaves, as well as any flowers or buds. Knock each plant out of its pot and check the root ball — earwigs often hide in the soil near the drainage holes.

When spraying is necessary, be sure to employ a product recommended for use in the house or greenhouse. Most garden chemicals are unsafe to use inside the house, where you will breathe in the fumes or handle treated plants. Always follow the instructions on the product label.

If possible, take infested plants into the garden for spraying; most chemicals, however safe, smell unpleasant and can stain fabrics. Wear rubber gloves (and all other protective gear called for on the product label) and wash your hands afterward.

◀ **Mite damage** Mites are serious plant pests and difficult to control, as they live within buds and leaf tissues. A badly infested hyacinth shows unsightly, discolored flowers.

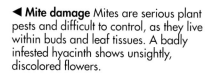

▼ **Scale insects** These troublesome pests, which attack houseplants, are often first noticed when leaves become sticky. The minute pests form brown, yellow, or white scales, which disfigure the leaves and sap a plant's energy.

PESTS

Most indoor pests are tiny, so inspect all houseplants regularly — don't wait until the symptoms are obvious; it may be too late. When repotting plants, pay attention to the roots, which can harbor the larvae (grubs) of many insects, as well as some adult pests. Underground pests often go undetected until the plant collapses.

Leaf and stem pests can be grouped according to their method of attack on plants. Mites and aphids suck the sap, causing yellowing or distorted growth; they often leave a sticky or sooty deposit on the foliage. Chewing insects bite stems and leaf edges or eat holes in the leaves. And the larvae of some insects bore tunnels, or "mines," in the leaves just below the surface.

Early detection of pests will usually enable you to curtail the problem with biological controls or relatively harmless products, such as insecticidal soap or horticultural oil. If these are inadequate, try any of a number of chemical pesticides approved for houseplants. These come in concentrated form for dilution as a spray, in aerosol cans, or even as granules for application to the potting soil.

APHIDS

Symptoms Colonies of small, round green, pinkish, yellow, or black sap-sucking insects, mostly wingless but with some winged individuals present. Stems, leaves, and flower buds rapidly become distorted, sticky, and weak.
Treatment Cut off and destroy badly infested growth. Spray with insecticidal soap.

CATERPILLARS

Symptoms Caterpillars chew leaves, making holes or notched edges. Some spin leaves together with silk threads. They rarely derive from eggs laid indoors but can be brought into the home on plants moved in from the greenhouse or garden.
Treatment Pick off and destroy individual caterpillars.

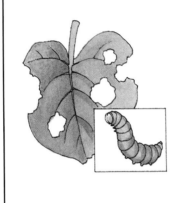

EARWIGS

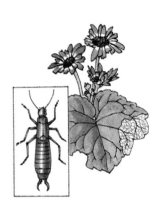

Symptoms Dark reddish-brown, narrow-bodied, ¾-1 in (2-2.5 cm) long insects, each with a pair of pincers at the tail, chew ragged holes in leaves and flowers. They feed at night, remaining hidden under leaves, in flowers, or in the potting soil during the day.
Treatment Shake earwigs out of plants and destroy them by hand.

FUNGUS GNATS

Symptoms Minute gnatlike flies (also called mushroom flies or sciarids) lay eggs in potting soil. Though usually harmless, their white, black-headed maggots sometimes eat roots, weakening growth. They are most troublesome in very moist, acid soils.
Treatment Repot into fresh potting mix or drench the potting soil with insecticide; avoid overwatering.

LEAF MINERS

Symptoms Slender sap-sucking maggots burrow or "mine" through leaf tissues just below the surface, creating a network of pale markings and weakening growth. Cinerarias and chrysanthemums are particularly susceptible to attack.
Treatment Pick off and destroy individual mined leaves; apply a recommended systemic insecticide, such as disulfoton.

MEALYBUGS

Symptoms Small, oval bugs covered with a whitish cottony secretion form colonies on stems and leafstalks, especially in sheathed leaf axils. Foliage turns yellow, wilts, and may fall.
Treatment Wipe off bugs with a damp cloth or with a cotton swab dipped in alcohol; spray with light superior horticultural oil.

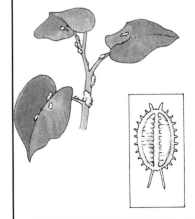

MITES

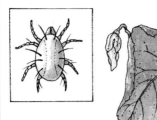

Symptoms Minute sap-sucking insects lay eggs in vast quantities, giving leaves and flower stems the appearance of being coated with dust. Leaves and flower stems become twisted, brittle, and scabby; buds wither; and open flowers lose their color. Attacks can often be fatal unless dealt with quickly. The mite most usually found indoors is the cyclamen mite, which attacks many other houseplants, including African violets, begonias, impatiens, gloxinias, ivies, and pelargoniums.

Treatment Pick off and destroy all infested leaves, buds, and flowers. Wash plants with soapy water or spray with insecticidal soap; or spray repeatedly with light superior horticultural oil or pyrethrin until all eggs and mites are destroyed. Maintain adequate humidity.

RED SPIDER MITES

Symptoms Minute reddish sap-sucking insects spin fine, silky webs mainly on the undersides of leaves, which become mottled, turn yellow, curl up, and fall. Hot, dry conditions encourage attack.

Treatment Cut off badly infested areas; spray repeatedly with insecticidal soap or light superior horticultural oil; mist daily with tepid water.

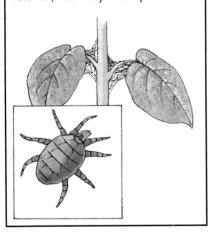

SCALE INSECTS

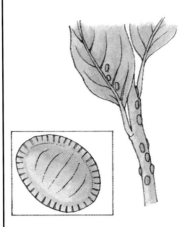

Symptoms Small brown or yellowish motionless scales — each of which covers a sap-sucking insect — infest stems and veins on leaf undersides, causing stickiness and withering.

Treatment Wipe off with a damp cloth or with a cotton swab soaked in alcohol; or spray with neem or light superior horticultural oil.

SYMPHYLANS

Symptoms Tiny, creamy white centipede-like creatures eat small roots and burrow inside larger roots, causing loss of vigor, wilting, and leaf drop. This pest is found only in unsterilized potting soils.

Treatment Use sterilized potting soil.

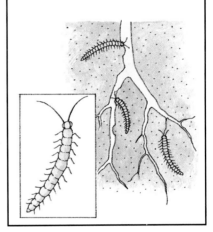

THRIPS

Symptoms Tiny black, feathery-winged jumping insects suck sap from soft tissues. Leaves become mottled or streaked; flowers develop white spots. Blobs of reddish excretion turn black, dirtying leaves and flowers.

Treatment Pick off and destroy damaged leaves and flowers; spray with insecticidal soap.

VINE WEEVILS

Symptoms Creamy white, ⅓ in (8 mm) long, fat grubs eat roots and tubers, causing rapid wilting and plant death. Adult beetlelike weevils chew holes in leaves.

Treatment Pick off and destroy adults. Drench soil with beneficial nematodes, but once the symptoms are evident it is usually too late to save the plant.

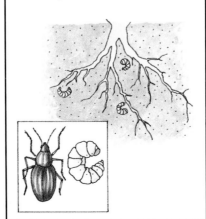

WHITEFLIES

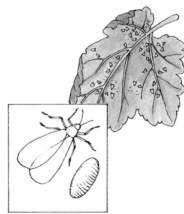

Symptoms Tiny, white mothlike flies infest the undersides of leaves, flying away when disturbed. Their whitish scalelike larvae suck sap and excrete sticky honeydew. Severe infestations weaken growth and cause yellowing.

Treatment Spray repeatedly with insecticidal soap, light superior horticultural oil, or pyrethrin.

DISEASES

Plant diseases result from infection by fungi, bacteria, or viruses. Since diseases are contagious, good hygiene is the best preventive measure. In addition, space plants well apart so that there is a free passage of air between them. Moist, stagnant air encourages the spread of many fungal diseases.

Remove any unhealthy-looking or dead material as soon as possible. Also remove bruised or damaged leaves. Always use sterile potting soils, since soilborne diseases can be very troublesome. Never use untreated garden soil for potting and always wash plastic or clay pots with a strong disinfectant before reusing them.

As with insecticides, if you decide to use chemicals for the control of houseplant diseases, do not choose those recommended solely for garden plants — they may be quite noxious indoors. In any case, it is best to take the plants outdoors before treating them. Fixed copper, benomyl, Bordeaux mixture, and sulfur can be used safely, and treated plants may be brought back indoors as soon as the leaves are dry and the smell has gone.

CROWN AND STEM ROT

Symptoms Stems become soft and slimy. Crown-forming plants such as African violets are attacked at the center by this fungal disease, which causes leaves to rot.
Treatment Cut away diseased stems, dusting wounds with sulfur; destroy all badly affected plants. Avoid overwatering, low temperature, and poor ventilation.

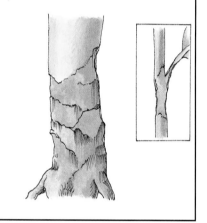

GRAY MOLD (botrytis)

Symptoms Fleshy leaves, stems, and flowers covered with fluffy gray mold, causing stunting.
Treatment Cut away affected growth, dusting wounds with sulfur; destroy badly affected plants. Treat minor outbreaks with fungicide. Avoid high humidity; don't wet leaves when watering; and improve ventilation.

LEAF SPOT

Symptoms Brown or yellowish spots on leaves, sometimes with a moist central area. Spots may enlarge and merge, killing the entire leaf.
Treatment Cut off and destroy affected leaves; spray with fungicide and reduce watering until cured. Don't allow water to settle on the leaves.

POWDERY MILDEW

Symptoms White powdery fungus coating or spotting leaves and stems. Flowers are sometimes also affected. Soft-leaved plants are most susceptible. Unlike gray mold, mildew is not fluffy.
Treatment Cut off and destroy affected leaves and stems; spray with fungicide. Improve ventilation.

ROOT ROT

Symptoms Leaves turn yellow, wilt, and fall. Roots become slimy. Symptoms may not appear until it is too late to save the plant.
Treatment Remove the plant from its pot, and shake away all soil. Cut away diseased roots, dust the rest with sulfur, then repot. Destroy badly affected plants. Avoid overwatering.

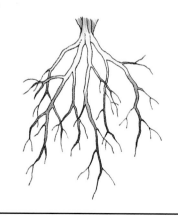

SOOTY MOLD

Symptoms Unsightly black fungus growing on the sticky honeydew secreted by aphids and other sap-sucking pests. Leaf pores become clogged and light is blocked out, reducing growth.
Treatment Wipe leaves with a cloth soaked in warm water; rinse with more water. Control honeydew-secreting pests.

DISORDERS

Many times houseplants display signs of ill health, but no evidence of pest or disease attack can be detected. The problem is likely to be associated with poor cultural conditions. In fact, most houseplant troubles are caused by incorrect watering or temperature control, and by drafts, dry air, inadequate nutrients, cramped roots, poor light, or too much direct sunlight.

Remember that plants that are grown indoors in temperate regions often grow in very different environments in the wild. These conditions must be matched as closely as possible if the plants are to remain healthy.

Unfortunately, houseplants vary enormously in their origins, and you may have inadvertently chosen to group together plants with widely differing likes and dislikes. The section "Identifying Houseplants" on pages 56–102 of this book will help you assemble plants in compatible groups.

If any of the symptoms featured below occur on your houseplants, trim away any growth that has been permanently damaged and take measures to overcome the cause of the problem — for example, by moving the plant.

BROWN BLOTCHES

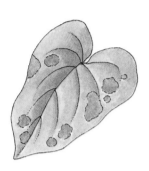

Symptoms Brown or discolored blotches or spots on leaves.
Causes Areas of dark brown soft tissue may be caused by overwatering. Pale brown crisp tissue is a sign of underwatering. Pale blotches often appear when cold water settles on the leaves or if plants are inadvertently sprayed with cosmetic aerosols, such as hair sprays.

BROWN EDGES OR TIPS

Symptoms Leaf edges or tips turn brown.
Causes Brown or yellow edges are a sign of too much or too little water, sun scorch or poor light, wrong temperature, overfeeding, too dry air, or drafts. If only the leaf tips turn brown *(inset)*, the cause may be dry air or a buildup of fertilizer or salt in the soil.

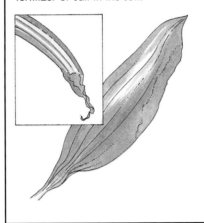

CURLING LEAVES

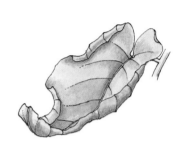

Symptoms Leaves curl up along their edges and eventually fall.
Causes If this disorder occurs in winter, the cause is probably cold drafts or generally too low temperatures. Overwatering can cause similar symptoms at any time of year. Unfurl the leaves to check for small leaf-rolling caterpillars.

DRIED-UP LEAVES

Symptoms Leaves dry up, turn brown all over, and eventually fall.
Causes If the plant is close to a heater or radiator, the cause is scorching. Elsewhere in the room the cause may be underwatering, insufficient daylight, or too high temperatures combined with lack of humidity.

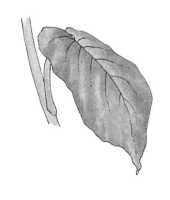

FLOWER BUDS FALL

Symptoms Plump, seemingly healthy flower buds fall off before they open.
Causes Underwatering, erratic watering, dry air, and a sudden change in growing conditions are all common causes of bud fall. Insufficient daylight results in poor flower production and bud abortion.

NO FLOWERS

Symptoms Generally healthy plants refuse to produce flowers.
Causes Insufficient light is a common cause. Some plants require a precise length of daylight for flower initiation. Overfeeding may encourage leaf growth at the expense of flowers. Many cacti need a period of dry rest at cooler temperatures before they will flower.

SLOW OR POOR GROWTH

Symptoms Plants fail to develop at the rate expected during the normal growing season.
Causes Underfeeding or insufficient daylight are common causes. Overwatering can also slow growth. Knock the plant out of its pot and check that it is not pot-bound — if it is, repot the plant in a larger container with fresh potting soil. Dust can clog leaf pores, especially those with a felted or hairy surface, preventing them from breathing properly.

Do not expect active growth during a northern winter — many plants go into a period of dormancy during that season's low temperatures and poor light, but this is not a sign of illness. Remember, too, that some types of plants, such as cacti, woody-stemmed shrubs, and many tropical palms, are naturally slow growing.

SPINDLY GROWTH

Symptoms Abnormally tall, soft growth with thin stems and pale leaves.
Causes Underfeeding or insufficient light is usually the cause during the normal active growth period. In a northern winter, when plants should be dormant, excess warmth may stimulate growth while there is too little light.

SUDDEN LEAF FALL

Symptoms Leaves fall off, with no previous signs of ailment.
Causes The plant's metabolism receives a shock — perhaps from a sudden change in light intensity, temperature, or water supply. Repotting into too large a pot can also cause stress. Cold air and shock during transit can defoliate plants fresh from the nursery.

VARIEGATION LOSS

Symptoms Plants that should have variegated or colored foliage develop all-green leaves on new growth.
Causes Insufficient light is the sole cause. Affected leaves cannot be restored to their correct color, so remove them. Given more light, subsequent growth should be variegated.

WILTING

Symptoms Leaves become limp; shoots or entire plants may keel over.
Causes Underwatering is a common cause, but overwatering can also be to blame. If the symptoms occur only around midday during summer, too much sun and heat are the causes. Also check that the plant is not pot-bound.

YELLOW LOWER LEAVES

Symptoms Mature leaves at the base of the plant turn yellow and eventually fall.
Causes Many species shed basal leaves as that foliage reaches the end of its active life. If several leaves fall at once, overwatering or a cold draft is probably to blame.

YELLOW NEW LEAVES

Symptoms The leaves on all new growth are abnormally yellow but otherwise healthy.
Causes The plant is probably an acid lover, in which case the cause is alkalinity in the soil caused by irrigation with hard (lime-rich) water. Repot into an acidic (peat-enriched) mix and irrigate with rainwater or distilled water.

SUITABLE CONTAINERS

**Almost any container can be used to display
plants, and decorative items originally designed for quite
different purposes are often the most eye-catching.**

Every indoor plant has two basic requirements — a growing medium, usually potting soil, and a container to hold it. Ordinary garden soil is unsuitable for houseplants, partly because it may harbor weed seedlings, pests, and disease spores, and partly because it may be short of nutrients and not have the structure to provide adequate drainage and water-holding capacity.

Potting media

Potting mix serves three main purposes — to hold a reserve of water, to supply nutrients, and to provide anchorage for the plants. While the potting mix remains moist, air can still circulate freely between the soil particles to prevent waterlogging.

There are many premixed potting soils available commercially, but for a more precise control of ingredients you may prefer to mix your own. Different types of plants prefer different potting mixes, and the same plant may prefer different mixes at different stages in its development. For example, seeds are commonly sown into seed-starting mix, which is largely composed of finely sifted sphagnum peat and perlite or vermiculite; but as the seedlings mature, they should be transferred to a standard potting mix of loam, coarse sand or perlite, and a coarser sphagnum peat. In any case, a homemade potting soil should always be sterilized by moistening it, placing it in a covered ovenproof pan, and then heating it in a 180° F (82° C) oven for an hour.

Plants with special needs may benefit from cultivation in specially formulated mixes that you can buy. These are named with the plant group; orchid mix or cactus mix are examples.

Soilless or peat-based mixes are naturally sterile but must be kept moist at all times. If they dry out, they shrink and leave a space between the root ball and the pot, allowing water to run out without

---

▼ **Stylish containers** Choose decorative containers that complement particular types of plants and suit the style of a room. These elegant planters and pots appear tailor-made for their occupants, each adding to the charm of the other.

▲ **Cascading greenery** A waterfall of variegated tradescantia spills out of the fountain, while the bird cage has become home to the feathery fronds of asparagus fern.

▼ **Colorful brew** A collection of teapots makes a charmingly off-beat setting for small flowering plants. These plants are actually growing in plastic pots, so they can easily be slipped out of the teapots and replaced when the flowers fade.

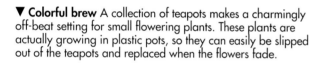

▲ **Plant display** Many ornaments, especially those with a gardening theme, make charming containers. This emerald feather (*Asparagus densiflorus* 'Sprengeri'), mulched with small pebbles, looks entirely natural in its handcrafted ceramic wheelbarrow.

◀ **Wicker baskets** The pleasing soft brown colors of wicker baskets complement flowering and foliage plants alike. Choose shapes to suit plant types — tubs for tulips, oval baskets for a collection of primulas, and square baskets for chrysanthemums and trailing ivies.

▲ **Trailing houseplants** Pedestals are ideal for displaying trailing houseplants, such as the wandering Jew (*Tradescantia fluminensis*). The green- and white-striped cultivar 'Quicksilver' shown here grows especially fast.

▶ **Unusual containers** This whimsical group includes such unconventional containers as a cat's feeding bowl for mauve campanulas and an old hatbox supporting a yucca.

▲ **Victorian jardiniere** A fixture in Victorian-style parlors, the highly glazed jardiniere consists of a large decorative plant bowl on a tall matching pedestal. Authentic pots have a small inner ledge near the base of the bowl on which a plant pot can rest, allowing surplus water to drain into the cavity below.

Such elaborately decorated containers demand dramatic plant displays — here, a mature spider plant *(Chlorophytum comosum)* drapes slender green- and white-striped leaves amid long flowering stems set with young plantlets.

▲▶ **Parlor palm** One of the easiest houseplants to grow, the parlor palm *(Chamaedorea elegans)* is an elegant foliage plant that tolerates poor light, air pollution, and normal room temperatures. It does object, though, to dry air. It can be misted, but it is easier to stand it in a deep container on a layer of constantly moist pebbles.

▶ **Macramé hanger** Available ready-made or in kit form, macramé hangers, fringed or trimmed with knotted cord, are ideal for displaying trailing houseplants. They should be suspended from sturdy hooks to take the combined weight of plants and moist potting mix, and positioned where they do not get in the way.

any benefit to the plant. Such soilless mixes should be potted loosely, never tamped down.

Choosing the correct pot size
Many popular houseplants grow to enormous sizes in their natural habitats. In the home, however, they remain manageable because their roots are restricted within pots. Eventually, a plant will exhaust the potting mix in which it is growing and fill the pot with a dense ball of roots that cannot absorb water or nutrients. Top growth becomes thin and lanky, and leaves wilt and fall off. Revive the plant by knocking it out of its present pot — easiest to do when the root ball is moist — and either repotting it or potting it on to a larger container.

Repotting is for plants that have reached their desired size but are in need of fresh potting mix. Remove at least a quarter of the existing ball of roots and soil, cutting off all dead roots before setting the plant in a clean pot of the same size and filling in with fresh potting mix. It can be impractical and awkward to repot large established plants in heavy, unwieldy containers. It is usually sufficient to scrape off the top of the old soil and replace it with new material.

Potting on annually at the start of the growing season is for a plant that has not reached its mature size. There is no need to reduce the root ball, except for the removal of dead root tissue. The plant should be moved to the next larger pot size and given new potting mix.

Clay and plastic pots
Standard clay or plastic pots are measured by the diameter of the rim, from 1½ in (4 cm) up to 15 in (38 cm) or more. Sizes move up by about ½ in (1 cm). Some popular sizes for houseplants are 3½ in (9 cm), 5 in (13 cm), and 7 in (18 cm). Tall-growing shrubs and climbers need much larger tubs.
Clay pots are usually unglazed. They are heavier than plastic pots

and are less likely to be knocked over, especially with tall plants grown in a lightweight compost. Clay pots "breathe" through the pores, and water evaporates from the side walls, so that the potting mix dries out quickly with little or no risk of waterlogging. These

pots are good for plants that enjoy dry conditions, such as cacti. Before using a clay pot, you should add a shallow layer of clay pot shards, clean pebbles, or stones to its bottom to enhance the drainage of water from the potting mix.

▶ **Contemporary decor** Modern trends in interior design call for clear, uncluttered shapes and plain, often bold colors. A collection of food cans holds an array of flowering and foliage plants, their bright labels evoking a sense of light-hearted fun.

◀ **Spring indoors** For a more garden-like display, force bulbs of different types together. Here a violet-colored hyacinth blooms among daffodils, tall *Anemone blanda*, and even a tuft of grass. The simple glass and plastic containers used here combine well. At the same time, the colors of the plastic pots make a perfect foil for the striking blossoms of compact primulas to the front and lower right.

▼ **Decorative cookware** Cake pans of every shape and size can make showy containers for houseplants. Aluminum types do not rust, but it is worth lining them with plastic to keep water from dribbling through the seams. For the best results, leave the plants in their plastic pots and set them on a base of pebbles to prevent waterlogging.

▲ **Terra-cotta bowls** The earthy color and simple beauty of unglazed terra-cotta pots and bowls combine well with the greenery of foliage plants. Decorative cereals and grasses are easy to raise from seed and produce lush foliage plants, which can be trimmed with scissors like miniature lawns.

Plastic pots are much cheaper than clay pots, less likely to break even though they are quite brittle, and come in varied colors and shapes. They are also easier than clay to keep clean, but because they are lightweight, they topple over easily. Also, as they are nonporous, they easily become waterlogged. Plastic pots have drainage holes and do not need a layer of drainage materials in the bottom.

Decorative containers Some clay pots are glazed, meaning that water does not evaporate through the sides. They are more attractive than unglazed pots and can be used as plant containers or as covers to hide practical but homely plastic pots.

Eye-catching decorative containers for plants can be created from household items designed for entirely different purposes. Copper and other cookware; porcelain, china, and glass containers; baskets; ceramic bowls; old teapots; and brass coal scuttles are all suitable, and they can be swapped to suit a change in mood or interior decor.

Unusual containers can reflect the function of a room. For example, aluminum baking trays, copper cooking pots, and decorative serving bowls can be transformed into display containers for houseplants in a kitchen. Old-fashioned tea and food tins can also be turned into plant pots, while glass or plastic candy jars can become bottle gardens.

Glass containers

The visual qualities of the potting mix are generally unimportant, because it is usually hidden in an opaque pot. But when growing plants in transparent glass bowls, you may wish to hide or replace the standard potting mix with a decorative material.

Gravel or pebbles are ideal embellishments for the rooting medium. These are available in shades of cream, gray, brown, or white. However, these materials will not meet the water- and nutrient-

holding requirements of a growing medium. When water is added, it fills all the air spaces between the pebbles and suffocates the roots, so they must be used in combination with a conventional potting mix.

There are two exceptions to this rule of thumb — bulbs and water plants. Bulbs have a built-in supply of nutrients, and provided the bulb itself is kept fairly dry (so that it won't rot) the roots will tolerate standing in waterlogged conditions (see pages 33–36). True water plants, such as the umbrella sedges (*Cyperus*), grow well in pebbles and water.

The roots of all other houseplants need air as well as water and nutrients. Prepare a decorative glass container by building up the walls with pebbles or gravel, then fill in the center with ordinary potting mix. Position the plants in the potting mix and cover the surface with more pebbles.

Another approach is to build layers of different-colored gravels, beginning with a generous layer of ordinary potting mix in the bottom, into which the plants can root. The overall effect is similar to looking at a geological cross-section.

Displaying houseplants

There's more to displaying houseplants than simply putting them in pots and standing them on a handy shelf or windowsill. Different styles are determined by how the plants relate to their containers and how the containers in turn relate to the room decor.

Try to match the style of the container with that of the plant. Bold designs complement the odd structure of such houseplants as yucca, Peruvian apple cactus (*Cereus uruguayense* 'Monstrosus'), flaming-sword (*Vriesea splendens*), and Norfolk Island pine (*Araucaria heterophylla*).

▶ **Indoor water garden** Natural water plants — *Cyperus, Scirpus,* and *Carex* species — look effective in glass bowls and tanks. Provide sand, gravel, or pebble beds for them to root into, with a few large stones for interest. Bulbs grow readily in special water-filled bulb vases.

▲ **Glass containers** In these see-through containers, the growing medium can become as much a part of the display as the plants. Here, contrasting layers of aggregate and potting soil create a striking base for vivid primulas, hyacinths, and narcissi.

◀ **Houseplant cuttings** Many cuttings will root in water, especially those from plants with embryonic root nodules on the stems, such as pothos and impatiens. When placed in a decorative glass or jar, such cuttings can look just as effective for a short spell as an established plant.

▼ **Desert cacti** Use decorative materials — gravel, small rocks, and pieces of driftwood — to create a desert scene for small, slow-growing cacti and succulents of contrasting form.

China containers are ideal for displaying filigree ferns; wicker baskets are good for displaying flowering plants and climbers like Cape leadwort *(Plumbago auriculata)*, white jasmine *(Jasminum officinale)*, Madagascar jasmine *(Stephanotis floribunda)*, and wax plant *(Hoya carnosa)*.

Grouping houseplants

Houseplants grow better when grouped together — benefiting from the increased local humidity created by a mass of foliage growing above a relatively large surface area of moist potting mix. However, if you want to grow several plants in the same container — especially if it is a small one — make sure that they all have similar requirements for light, water, and nutrition and that they grow slowly. Vigorous plants will choke others in the container.

Any type of bowl can be used, provided it is reasonably deep — very shallow ones dry out too quickly. Many garden centers offer a range of quite cheap but pretty china planters, or you can opt for a more expensive terracotta or glazed ceramic type.

A bowl with drainage holes in the bottom will need a matching saucer or drip tray. One without holes should be partly filled with a suitable drainage material — pebbles, clay shards, or perlite, with some charcoal to keep it sweet — before filling to the top with potting mix.

Growing plants in containers without drainage, however, is a commitment to extra care. You will have to water carefully, since excess water cannot drain away. In addition, you will have to repot more often, since excess salts and fertilizers will not be able to wash out of the soil through the bottom of the pot. In the end, you may prefer to use drainerless containers as a shell, to hold and conceal standard pots.

Baskets should be lined with a watertight material, such as black polyethylene film, before planting, but don't make any drainage holes in the bottom of the liner — water will ruin the basket.

To plant a mixed bowl or basket, either knock each plant out of its original pot and replant it in the potting soil, or keep some or all the plants in their individual pots and sink them in moist peat moss in the container.

Flowering plants are best kept in their own separate pots, so that they can be removed easily from the arrangement once the flowers have faded without disturbing the roots of the others. For a table decoration or other short-term arrangement, just spread a layer of fresh sphagnum moss around the rims of the pots.

The most attractive displays offer a range of growth habits, leaf shapes, and colors. Use upright plants with bold or spiky leaves to produce height and scale. Bushier plants will fill in the bulk of the container, and trailers such as ivy will break up the hard edges. If the display is to be viewed from one side only, stagger the plants in descending tiers, preferably with the tallest one positioned off-center. For a table centerpiece, put the tallest plant in the middle of the display.

Plants with stunning foliage — such as rex begonias, coleuses, and marantas — often look better on their own, but several of the same species can be put in one bowl or basket to increase their overall size and impact. A simple arrangement in a plain container can be as eye-catching as a lavish one in an ornate container — the choice is yours. If you wish, add polished stones, some wood bark, or even a ribbon bow for a final decorative touch.

▲ **China bowls** The colors and shapes of containers are important in group arrangements. White bowls are perfect for such bright flowers as purple-flowered *Exacum affine*, bush violet *(Browallia speciosa)*, orange-red kalanchoe, and miniature red-berried bead plant *(Nertera granadensis)*. A grassy-leaved sweet flag *(Acorus gramineus)* provides an elegant backdrop.

▼ **Basket plants** A group arrangement of contrasting foliage is always eye-catching. Here, the soft green fronds of maidenhair fern *(Adiantum capillus-veneris)* add airy charm to the more substantial leaves of pink-marbled polka-dot plant *(Hypoestes)* and the thick, hairy leaves of African violet.

▲ **African violets** Trimmed here with strands of ivy, African violets (*Saintpaulia*) have single or double flowers, often with frilly petals. These low-growing plants enjoy close planting for extra humidity. Set them on a layer of moist pebbles in a shallow bowl.

◀ **Spring basket** A lined basket holds a bright spring display of golden cyclamineus narcissi and white polyanthus primulas. Green and variegated ivies tumble over the moss-covered edges.

▼ **Colored foliage** Rich leaf colors develop best in bright but filtered light. Marbled *Begonia rex*, white-spotted *Dieffenbachia maculata*, and trailing yellow-variegated pothos all have identical light requirements. A fruit-laden calamondin orange (x *Citrofortunella mitis*) does best in full sun and adds a bright spot of color to the group.

Identifying houseplants

The individual leaf shapes and colors of houseplants often provide a good indication of their cultural needs. The large *Ficus* genus, for example, includes the trailing or climbing *F. pumila,* whose thin-textured miniature leaves require a high degree of humidity, and the treelike rubber plant *(F. elastica),* whose leathery leaves tolerate much drier air conditions. Both grow well in subdued light, but variegated forms of the rubber plant, such as 'Doescheri' and 'Tricolor,' develop ivory and pink markings only in bright though filtered light.

All plants with variegated and colored foliage need well-lit positions, as do flowering and scented plants, though they also require some protection from hot midday summer sun. The only indoor plants that revel in full sun are desert cacti and some leaf succulents. Large-leaved and thick-textured plants are probably the easiest to accommodate — *Aspidistra*, for example, is virtually indestructible, tolerating less than ideal conditions, including shade and dry air.

Some families of plants, such as palms and ferns, are easily recognized by their finely divided leaf fans and fronds. These two groups have almost identical needs, though ferns demand particularly good humidity. The distinctive bromeliads, with their colorful vases of foliage and exotic flower bracts, are in a class of their own, but they are no more difficult to care for than other vividly colored houseplants.

Leaf identification Houseplants range from tiny-leaved miniatures to needlelike leaf sprays and bold jungle exotics.

TINY-LEAVED HOUSEPLANTS

**Small-leaved plants fit neatly on
windowsills and tabletops, and many are perfect
for miniature and bottle gardens.**

Plants with flowers and large, bold leaves are popular for indoor use, but many tiny-leaved plants display even more interesting features — delicate leaf shapes and textures, trailing or creeping stems, color patterns, and unusual flowers and fruits. Their charm can be appreciated only by taking a close-up look, though by grouping several plants even the smallest foliage can be eye-catching. While unsuitable for large, floor-level containers, tiny-leaved plants are ideal for shelf displays, table arrangements, and hanging baskets.

The container size should be related to the plant size for all types of houseplants, but it is even more important to choose a container of the right proportions when growing miniature plants, creepers, or trailers.

Very-low-growing plants are best grown in shallow azalea pots, bulb pans, and bowls, and they can be used as "ground cover" below a larger plant in a full-size pot. Trailing plants are excellent for hanging baskets or wall-mounted containers, or they may be used to break up the solid edges of a larger container filled with larger plants.

With a little artistic flair, you can create a miniature garden. Select a broad bowl or trough with a depth of about 3-4 in (7.5-10 cm). Cover the bottom with a 1 in (2.5 cm) layer of gravel or coarse perlite for good drainage, then fill to the top with ordinary potting mix. Draw up a plan of the desired planting — as you would for an outdoor garden — including pieces of wood bark, stones, or other decorative items.

Insert the chosen plants one at a time, starting at the center and working outward. You may need to trim some of the plants from time to time if you are growing several plants of differing vigor within one container.

Many small-leaved plants need quite humid air conditions in order to thrive. To humidify, set each pot on a saucer filled with gravel, and keep the gravel constantly moist — the air around the small plants will then be adequately humid. A northern winter, with its artificially hot and dry indoor atmosphere, can take a toll on these plants; in that situation they are best grown in a terrarium. Daily spraying with tepid water also increases humidity, but do not spray hairy or felted leaves.

The following pages offer advice on each of the most popular tiny-leaved species. The sizes given refer to *height × spread* unless otherwise stated.

◀ **Shelf display** Small-leaved plants show up better when grown in company rather than as isolated specimens. Their diversity in shape, color, and growth habit becomes truly apparent within an assorted group of plants. Here, trailers, including gray-green string-of-beads (*Senecio rowleyanus*), rosary vine (*Ceropegia woodii*) with its purple-flushed heart-shaped leaves, and *Sedum sieboldii* 'Medio-variegatum' (bottom shelf), tumble among cacti and ferns.

Adiantum capillus-veneris
Southern maidenhair fern

Features Delicate-looking fern with light green fronds comprising many fan-shaped leaflets (pinnae) on arching, blackish hairlike stalks.
Size 10 × 10 in (25 × 25 cm).
Needs Medium to bright indirect light; moist air (mist daily during hot spells); normal room temperature; water moderately; use half-strength fertilizer once in spring, once in summer.

Bowiea volubilis
Climbing onion

Features Thin, twining stems with sparse, short-lived leaves clamber from a surface bulb. Tiny greenish flowers in spring.
Size 1 ft (30 cm) or more tall.
Needs Bright light; normal room temperature and humidity; water moderately; use liquid fertilizer monthly during active growth.

Buxus microphylla
Box (small-leaved)

Features Bushy evergreen shrub similar to compact outdoor type. Oval, glossy dark green leaves. Variegated forms exist.
Size 9 × 6 in (23 × 15 cm).
Needs Bright light or semishade; normal room temperature and humidity; water moderately; use liquid fertilizer monthly in spring and summer. Prune to shape.

Ceropegia linearis woodii
Rosary vine

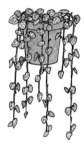

Features Long trailer growing from a surface tuber. Purplish threadlike stems bear sparse dark green, silver-marbled, heart-shaped leaves, colored purple beneath. Small pale pink and purple flowers in late summer.
Size Stems trail to 3 ft (90 cm).
Needs Strong light with some direct sun; normal room temperature and humidity; keep dry in winter; fertilize mature plants monthly during active growth; pot in cactus soil mix.

Crassula muscosa
Rattail crassula

Features Small multibranched succulent with slender, upright stems and minute pointed, fleshy leaves forming four-sided scaly columns. Insignificant green flowers.
Size 8 × 5 in (20 × 13 cm).
Needs Bright light with some direct sun; normal room temperature and humidity; water moderately during active growth; use liquid fertilizer every 2 weeks. Give winter rest at 50° F (10° C); water sparingly.

Crassula rupestris
Buttons-on-a-string

Features Small, spreading succulent, with the stem appearing to pass through the fleshy, almost triangular leaves like a string through beads. Small pink flowers in clusters at the ends of the stems in summer.
Size Stems to 2 ft (60 cm) long.
Needs Bright light with some direct sun; normal room temperature and humidity; use liquid fertilizer every 2 weeks during active growth.

Ficus pumila
Creeping fig

Features Multibranched species with wiry, trailing, or climbing stems; aerial roots cling to moist soil. Small, oval, pointed, glossy dark green and slightly puckered leaves, up to 1 in (2.5 cm) long. 'Minima' is more compact, with tiny leaves; 'Variegata' has cream edges.

Size 2 × 1 ft (60 × 30 cm).
Needs Filtered bright or medium light best but tolerates shade; humid air; cool to normal room temperature (winter rest at 50°F/10°C); water freely during growing season; give liquid fertilizer twice monthly. In winter, keep soil barely moist. Use peat-enriched soil. Pinch off growing tips on trailing plants to induce bushy habit.

Fittonia verschaffeltii argyroneura
Mosaic plant

Features Low-creeping plant; slightly pointed oval leaves, olive-green with network of silver-white veins.
Size 2 × 9 in (5 × 23 cm).
Needs Medium light with no direct sun, brighter in winter; normal constant room temperature (minimum 55°F/13°C); moist air; water regularly but sparingly; use half-strength liquid fertilizer every 2 weeks during active growth. Pinch growing tips to promote side shoots.

Glechoma/Nepeta hederacea
Ground ivy

Features Creeping perennial from Europe that is a weed in the garden but useful indoors for ground cover or in a hanging basket. Leaves are scalloped and slightly hairy.
Size Stems trail to 2 ft (60 cm).
Needs Light shade; normal room temperature and humidity; water moderately; use liquid fertilizer every 2 weeks during active growth.

Hedera helix cultivars
English ivy (small-leaved)

Features Trailing or climbing stems with lobed leaves — cultivars marked with cream or yellow.
Size Stems to 4 ft (1.2 m).
Needs Bright light best, green-leaved types tolerate light shade; normal room temperature and humidity; water moderately; give liquid fertilizer every 2 weeks during active growth.

Hypocyrta/Nematanthus

Features Upright or arching stems with glossy, rather fleshy dark green leaves and small, waxy orange, red, or yellow bell-shaped flowers in summer.
Size 1 × 1 ft (30 × 30 cm).
Needs Bright indirect light; normal room temperature; high humidity; water freely; give liquid fertilizer every 2 weeks during active growth. Water sparingly in winter. Pot into African violet mix.

Mimosa pudica
Sensitive plant

Features Branching plant with feathery leaves that fold in on themselves rapidly when touched. Leafstalks also bend, returning to their original position after a short time. Tiny pink flowers in summer.
Size 2 × 2 ft (60 × 60 cm).
Needs Bright light; normal room temperature; moist air; water moderately; apply high-potash liquid fertilizer every 2 weeks.

Nertera granadensis/depressa
Bead plant

Features Tiny, closely matted prostrate stems, rooting at the nodes. Midgreen fleshy leaves. Tiny yellow-green flowers. Shiny orange-red berries, ½ in (6 mm) in diameter.
Size 2 in (5 cm) high, spreading to width of container.
Needs Bright light with some direct sun; temperature 50°-59°F (10°-15°C); high humidity; water moderately all year; use liquid fertilizer monthly once flowers are over, until berries mature.

Pellaea rotundifolia
Button fern

Features Arching and eventually trailing fronds and brownish-black stalks closely set with pairs of small, almost round, leathery dark green leaflets. Rootstock is a shallow-growing, creeping rhizome. Moderately vigorous. Unlike any other fern in appearance.

Size Trails to 1 ft (30 cm), with a similar spread.
Needs Medium light, away from bright sun in summer. Humid air essential if above 61°F (16°C). Normal room temperature (winter minimum 50°F/10°C); keep potting mix moist in growing season; use dilute fertilizer every 2 weeks during active growth; water sparingly in cooler temperatures (50°F/10°C).

Peperomia rotundifolia 'Pilosior'
Yerba linda

Features Small trailing plant with tiny rounded leaves with faint brown alligator markings. Stems have reddish tinge. No flowers.
Size Stems trail to 8 in (20 cm).
Needs Light shade; normal room temperature (cool temperature in winter); moist air; water sparingly; apply dilute liquid fertilizer monthly during active growth. Grow in peat-enriched potting soil.

Pilea microphylla
Artillery plant

Features Fine midgreen foliage in flattened sprays — individual leaf fronds are ¼ in (6 mm) long. Inconspicuous greenish-yellow summer blooms expel clouds of pollen.
Size 1 × 1 ft (30 × 30 cm).
Needs Medium or bright indirect sun; moist, warm air; water sparingly; feed every 2 weeks during active growth only. Pot in peat-enriched mix; replace with cuttings as plants outgrow 4 in (10 cm) pots.

Pilea nummulariifolia
Creeping Charlie

Features Fast-growing creeper ideal for a hanging basket. Stems are thin and reddish with pale green quilted leaves. Flowers are insignificant.
Size Stems trail to 1 ft (30 cm).
Needs Semishade; normal room temperature (cool temperature in winter); moist, warm air; water moderately; use liquid fertilizer every 2 weeks from midspring to the end of summer.

Sedum/Hylotelephium sieboldii
October daphne

Features Succulent trailer with round, slightly toothed gray-green leaves, blotched creamy white in cultivar 'Medio-variegatum.' Clusters of pink flowers in fall.
Size Stems trail to 9 in (23 cm).
Needs Full sun; normal room temperature and humidity; water moderately; do not feed. Give winter rest at 50°F (10°C).

Selaginella species and cultivars
Little club moss

Features Mosslike, low mounding, creeping, or upright bushy plants with tiny leaves in ranks around stems, giving a fernlike appearance. Species and cultivars have green, yellow, or silvery white marked foliage.
Size 2-12 × 6-12 in (5-30 × 15-30 cm) according to cultivar.
Needs Medium to low light; warm room temperature; very moist air (mist daily); water plentifully; apply quarter-strength liquid fertilizer every 2 weeks during active growth. Best in a bottle garden.

Senecio rowleyanus
String-of-beads

Features Prostrate and trailing plant with fleshy stems bearing beadlike gray-green leaves. White, sweetly scented flowers.
Size Stems trailing to 2-3 ft (60-90 cm).
Needs Bright light with some direct sun; normal room temperature and humidity; water moderately during active growth, sparingly at other times; feed monthly during active growth. Pot in sandy cactus mix.

Soleirolia/Helxine soleirolii
Baby's tears

Features Low-creeping plant, also known as mind-your-own-business; makes good ground cover under larger plants, with fleshy pink stems that root as they grow. Tiny, densely set, rounded leaves are pale green to midgreen.
Size 3-4 in (7.5-10 cm) tall.

Needs Bright but filtered light or partial shade in summer; normal room temperature; moist air (mist daily with tepid water); water freely and use liquid fertilizer occasionally during active growth. Give winter rest at 39°-45°F (4°-7°C); water sparingly.

BOLD-LEAVED HOUSEPLANTS

**Large-leaved houseplants of sizable proportions
make stunning focal points in spacious living rooms,
large halls, and open stairwells.**

Adequate space is needed to display tall, large-leaved houseplants properly. But most homes have at least one corner that is ideal for a shrubby or even tree-like container plant. Large and open living rooms with French windows for good light and well-lit stairwells and landings are perfect settings for such sculptural plants.

A large plant requires a big pot to ensure physical stability, an adequate supply of nutrients and moisture to the roots, and well-shaped growth. Ceramic or terra-cotta pots are much heavier than plastic ones, so they provide steadier anchorage for top-heavy plants. Fill the pots with loam-based potting soils, which are heavier than soilless mixes.

Staking may be necessary to keep tall-growing species upright. Use a sturdy bamboo stake and secure the main stem or branches with soft cotton string or ready-made plastic plant ties.

For plants with aerial roots — such as Swiss-cheese plant *(Monstera)* and some philodendrons — insert a moss-covered pole into the potting soil to provide a moist support that will help to hold the plant upright. You can buy such poles at a garden center, or you can make your own. Use nylon fishing line to tie sphagnum moss around a length of 1-2 in (2.5-5 cm) diameter standard plumbing pipe.

Fasten the plant to the moss-padded pipe by tying in aerial roots with more fishing line. If the roots aren't tough enough for this treatment, gently secure the plant's main stems to the support with soft string. Spray the moss with water every few days to encourage the aerial roots to grow into the moss and to increase the immediate humidity.

Most large-leaved houseplants either do not flower or have insignificant blossoms. Those with dark, leathery leaves usually tolerate normal room conditions and don't require full sunlight. The types that do flower, such as *Strelitzia* and *Anthurium* species, do best in a plant-filled sunroom, where bright light can be combined with fairly high humidity.

The sizes given on the following pages refer to *height* × *spread* unless otherwise stated. The directions for watering and fertilization apply to seasons when the plant is actively growing (typically spring through fall); cease fertilization and reduce watering during semidormancy in winter. Recommendations for frequency of feeding presume the use of an ordinary liquid or water-soluble houseplant fertilizer mixed as directed on the product label.

▶ **Banyan tree** In its native habitat of India, the Banyan tree or East Indian fig tree *(Ficus benghalensis)* grows up to 100 ft (30 m) tall, but as an indoor container plant it rarely exceeds 8 ft (2.4 m). Related to the more common rubber plant, the Banyan tree's arching stems bear rich green leathery leaves covered in soft brown hairs.

Anthurium andraeanum
Flamingo lily

Features Deep green, glossy, heart-shaped leathery leaves up to 8 in (20 cm) long. Vivid red flower spathes from spring to fall.
Size 1½ × 1 ft (45 × 30 cm), taller with age.
Needs Filtered light; warm room temperature; high humidity; keep moist and feed monthly.

Calathea makoyana
Peacock plant

Features Silvery green upright leaves, 6 in (15 cm) long; veined, edged, and blotched with darker green; undersides patterned with red and purple. (See also page 68.)
Size 2 × 1½ ft (60 × 45 cm).
Needs Filtered light; normal room temperature; water and feed well.

Codiaeum variegatum pictum
Croton

Features Glossy leathery leaves up to 1 ft (30 cm) long, veined and patterned with yellow, orange, red, or purple, changing with age.
Size 3 × 2 ft (90 × 60 cm).
Needs Bright light, some full sun; normal room temperature; humid air; keep soil moist; feed every 2 weeks.

Dieffenbachia maculata
Spotted dumbcane

Features Elliptical to oblong, cream-marbled, glossy dark green leaves up to 1½ ft (45 cm) or more long on sturdy upright stalks. Poisonous; sap temporarily paralyzes tongue and throat if swallowed.
Size 2-4 × 2-3 ft (60-120 × 60-90 cm).
Needs Bright but filtered light; normal room temperature; humid air; water moderately; feed every 2 weeks.

Dracaena fragrans 'Massangeana'
Corn plant

Features Broadly strap-shaped, arching, rich green leaves up to 2 ft (60 cm) long, patterned with yellow central stripes.
Size Eventually up to 4 × 2½ ft (120 × 75 cm).
Needs Bright but filtered light; warm room temperature; humid air (mist daily); keep soil moist; feed every 2 weeks.

Fatsia japonica
Japanese fatsia

Features Glossy dark green leaves, 9 in (23 cm) or more wide, deeply divided into five to nine coarsely toothed lobes. 'Variegata' has white-edged leaves.
Size Up to 5 × 4 ft (1.5 × 1.2 m) or more according to pot size.
Needs Shade tolerant; normal room temperature or less; fresh air; keep moist; feed every 2 weeks.

Ficus benghalensis
Banyan tree, East Indian fig tree

Features Broadly oval, leathery dark green leaves up to 8 in (20 cm) or more long with yellowish veins. Young shoots covered with fine russet hair.
Size 6-8 × 2 ft (180-240 × 60 cm).
Needs Bright but filtered light; normal room temperature; water moderately; feed every 2 weeks.

Ficus elastica '**Decora**'
Rubber plant

Features Oval, leathery, glossy dark green leaves up to 1 ft (30 cm) long with a prominent midrib, usually on an unbranched stem.
Size Up to 10 × 3 ft (300 × 90 cm).
Needs Bright but filtered light; normal room temperature; water moderately; feed every 2 weeks.

Ficus lyrata
Fiddle-leaf fig

Features Rich green violin-shaped leaves, often over 1 ft (30 cm) long, with puckered and wavy edges.
Size 4-6 × 2-3 ft (120-180 × 60-90 cm).
Needs Bright but filtered light; normal room temperature; water moderately; feed every 2 weeks.

Monstera deliciosa
Swiss-cheese plant

Features Heart-shaped, glossy green leaves up to 1½ ft (45 cm) wide on long stalks. Mature plants produce deeply incised leaves, perforated with elongated holes, and trailing aerial roots.
Size Up to 10 × 6 ft (3 × 1.8 m).
Needs Bright but filtered light; normal room temperature; high humidity; keep soil slightly moist; feed every 2 weeks.

Musa acuminata '**Dwarf Cavendish**'
Dwarf banana

Features Paddle-shaped leaves with prominent midribs. Curious flowers and small banana fruits are produced only on mature greenhouse plants.
Size 4-6 × 5 ft (1.2-1.8 × 1.5 m).
Needs Bright but filtered light; warm room temperature; humid air; water well; feed every 2 weeks.

Philodendron angustisectum
Philodendron

Features Broad, glossy rich green leaves up to 15 in (38 cm) long, deeply cut into many fingerlike segments, borne on long stalks.
Size 4-6 × 4 ft (1.2-1.8 × 1.2 m).
Needs Medium light, shade tolerant; normal room temperature; humid air; keep soil moist in summer; feed every 2 weeks.

Philodendron bipinnatifidum
Philodendron

Features Broad, dark green, deeply incised leaves up to 2 ft (60 cm) long, borne on long stalks. Stems grow trunklike with age.
Size 4 × 4 ft (1.2 × 1.2 m).
Needs Bright but filtered light; normal room temperature; humid air; keep soil moist in summer; feed every 2 weeks.

Philodendron domesticum
Spearhead philodendron

Features Narrowly triangular to arrow-shaped, rich green, glossy leaves up to 2 ft (60 cm) long.
Size Up to 6 × 3½ ft (1.8 × 1.1 m).
Needs Bright but filtered light; normal room temperature; humid air; keep soil moist in summer; feed every 2 weeks.

Philodendron selloum
Saddle-leaved philodendron

Features Similar to *Philodendron bipinnatifidum,* but leaves are whole, usually shallowly lobed, with wavy edges.
Size Up to 6 × 4 ft (1.8 × 1.2 m).
Needs Bright but filtered light; normal room temperature; humid air; keep soil moist in summer; feed every 2 weeks.

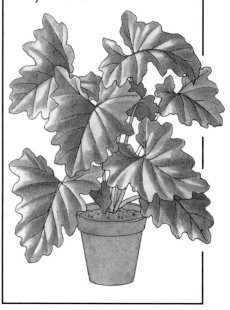

Schefflera/Brassaia actinophylla
Umbrella tree

Features Long-stalked, glossy rich green leaves, each divided umbrella-like into 4-16 separately stalked, arching, fingerlike leaflets.
Size 3-6 × 2-4 ft (90-180 × 60-120 cm).
Needs Bright to medium light; normal to warm room temperature; good humidity; keep soil slightly moist; feed every 2 weeks.

Spathiphyllum 'Mauna Loa'

Features Broadly lance-shaped to elliptical, glossy dark green leaves up to 9 in (23 cm) long, borne on slender stalks in clumps directly from the rhizome. Arumlike flowers backed by a creamy white saillike spathe appear on tall, slender stalks, mainly in spring, but often continuing intermittently until fall.
Size 2 × 2 ft (60 × 60 cm).
Needs Medium filtered light; normal room temperature; humid air; keep soil moist; feed every 2 weeks.

Strelitzia reginae
Bird-of-paradise

Features Paddlelike, gray-green, 15 in (38 cm) long leaves on long stalks. Exotic orange-and-blue flowers in spring or summer.
Size To 4 × 4 ft (120 × 120 cm).
Needs Bright light with direct sun; normal room temperature; keep soil moist in summer, dry in winter; feed every 2 weeks.

VARIEGATED FOLIAGE PLANTS

**The decorative effect of foliage in the home
can be heightened and dramatized by the endless patterns
offered by variegated and marbled plants.**

The green pigment, or chlorophyll, in the inner tissues of a plant's leaves carries out photosynthesis. This is the chemical process by which plants manufacture food substances using sunlight as the energy source. Chlorophyll is sometimes absent from part of the leaf, resulting in paler or darker patches. Such variegation can be highly decorative and is in many cases completely natural.

Sometimes the loss of chlorophyll is caused by a virus although this is more likely to occur on outdoor plants. The complete yellowing of leaves that are normally green is often due to chlorosis, especially when an acid-loving plant is grown in alkaline soil or irrigated with lime-rich tap water.

On most variegated leaves, the basic green is marked with white, gray, silver, cream, gold, or yellow. The patterns produced by variegations can be either simple or bold. Striped effects may occur from crossbanding, as in some dracaenas, or from longitudinal lines, as in tradescantias and sansevierias. Patterning can also follow the leaf veins — crotons and calatheas are typical of this type. The leaf edges of some plants may be heavily picked out in gold or silver, as in many ivies and peperomias. Other plants produce marbled leaves where cream or yellow areas appear as irregular blotches covering all or part of the leaf surface, as in dumbcanes and pothos.

Whether the differences in pattern have come about naturally or by skillful plant breeding, variegated foliage looks artistic and seems at home among household furnishings and fabrics. A variegated houseplant exists for every situation — whether you need a creeper, a bushy type, or a climber — though only a few flower as houseplants.

The lesser area of green tissue on variegated plants renders the plants less able to manufacture food substances than all-green plants, so the variegated plants are commonly less vigorous. To maintain healthy growth and good leaf color, variegated plants should be given more light. However, direct sunlight can be harmful, since the paler leaf areas are often prone to scorching. In summer, indirect but bright light or filtered sunlight is satisfactory.

If an all-green shoot appears on a variegated plant — called reversion — it will be more vigorous than the rest, creating an unbalanced shape. Prune the all-green growth immediately, cutting as close to its point of origin as possible.

Don't confuse reversion with loss of variegation due to insufficient light. Move the plant to a brighter spot — old leaves may not recover their full color, but new leaves will have the correct variegation.

The following pages review the most common variegated houseplants, giving the height and spread of mature specimens. Unless otherwise noted, watering and feeding instructions apply to periods of active growth. Feeding instructions presume the use of standard liquid or water-soluble houseplant fertilizer.

▶ **Leaf variegations** The patterns on houseplant foliage range from intricate markings to simple patches. They may marble almost the whole leaf in gold, white, or silver or shade in the leaf veins or edges with narrow bands of color. Variegated foliage plants look particularly dramatic when set against all-green types.

Abutilon pictum
Flowering maple

Features Vinelike, five-lobed leaves, 5 in (13 cm) wide, richly mottled yellow on dark green. Red-veined, salmon bell-shaped flowers in summer and fall.
Size Up to 4 × 3 ft (120 × 90 cm).
Needs Bright light, some full sun; cool room temperature in winter; water moderately (sparingly in winter); use liquid fertilizer every 2 weeks.

Aglaonema nitidum 'Silver Queen'
Chinese evergreen

Features Thick, leathery, dark gray-green leaves, heavily marbled with silvery cream, to 1 ft (30 cm) long, on thick, short stems. Flowers rare indoors.
Size Up to 2 × 1 ft (60 × 30 cm).
Needs Medium light, no direct sun; normal to warm room temperature; humid air; water moderately; use liquid fertilizer monthly.

Aphelandra squarrosa 'Louisae'
Zebra plant

Features Broad, fleshy, glossy dark green leaves, 9 in (23 cm) long, veined ivory-white. Small flowers in a conelike head with bright yellow bracts (often bought in bloom but may not repeat).
Size To 1½ × 1 ft (45 × 30 cm).
Needs Bright sunlight; warm room temperature; humid air; keep soil slightly damp; feed every 2 weeks during active growth.

Chlorophytum comosum 'Vittatum'
Spider plant

Features Grassy clump of soft, arching leaves, up to 1 ft (30 cm) long, medium green with central creamy white bands. Plantlets form at the ends of long, trailing stems. Flowers insignificant.
Size Up to 1 × 1½ ft (30 × 45 cm).
Needs Bright light or semishade; normal room temperature; water plentifully; feed every 2 weeks during active growth.

Codiaeum variegatum pictum
Croton

Features Bushy shrub with glossy, leathery, broad or narrow, sometimes incised leaves, up to 1 ft (30 cm) long, veined or marked with yellow, orange, red, or purple.
Size Up to 3 × 2 ft (90 × 60 cm).
Needs Bright light, some full sun; normal room temperature; humid air; keep soil moist (less so in winter); feed every 2 weeks.

Dieffenbachia species
Dumbcane

Features Broad, soft leaves up to 1 ft (30 cm) long, dark or pale green with white, cream, or yellowish blotchy markings or marbling, especially around the midrib (all parts poisonous).
Size 2-4 × 2-3 ft (60-120 × 60-90 cm).
Needs Bright but indirect light; minimum temperature 59°F (15°C); humid air; keep soil slightly damp; feed every 2 weeks.

Dracaena fragrans 'Massangeana'
Corn plant

Features Loosely arching, glossy green leaves, up to 2 ft (60 cm) long, each with a broad central stripe of yellow and usually one or two narrower yellow stripes alongside. A trunklike stem may form with age. 'Lindenii' has similar habit, but its leaves have broad, creamy gold marginal stripes.
Size Generally 2 × 2 ft (60 ×60 cm); up to 4 × 2½ ft (120 × 75 cm), growing with age.
Needs Bright but filtered light, no direct sun; warm room temperature; humid air (stand pot on saucer of moist pebbles; mist foliage frequently); keep soil moist (less so in winter); feed every 2 weeks during spring and summer.

Dracaena godseffiana/surculosa
Gold-dust dracaena

Features Dark green, cream-spotted, 3 in (7.5 cm) long, elliptical leaves in twos or threes up wiry stems. In some cultivars the spots merge to form solid patches.
Size Up to 24 × 15 in (60 × 38 cm).
Needs Bright but filtered light; warm room temperature; humid air; keep soil moist (less so in winter); feed every 2 weeks during active growth.

Dracaena sanderana
Belgian evergreen

Features Slender and upright, rarely branching. Rather stiff, deep green, white-margined leaves up to 9 in (23 cm) long and 1 in (2.5 cm) wide.
Size Up to 18 × 15 in (45 × 38 cm).
Needs Bright but filtered light; warm room temperature; humid air; keep soil moist (less so in winter); feed every 2 weeks.

Euonymus japonica 'Mediopicta'
Japanese spindle tree

Features Bushy with leathery, pointed-oval, yellow-centered, rich green leaves up to 2 in (5 cm) long.
Size To 2½ × 1½ ft (75 × 45 cm).
Needs Bright but filtered light (some full sun in winter, but protect from undue warmth); maximum temperature 65°F (18°C) in summer, 50°-55°F (10°-13°C) in winter; keep soil moist (less so in winter); feed every 2 weeks.

Hedera canariensis **and**
Hedera helix **cultivars**
Canary and English ivies

Features *H. canariensis* has large, triangular, slightly lobed leaves; 'Gloire de Marengo' *(shown)* has 3-4 in (7.5-10 cm) long leaves with gray-green patches and silver and white borders. *H. helix* has three- to five-lobed, 1-2 in (2.5-5 cm) long leaves; variegated cultivars, popular as houseplants, are 'Glacier' (gray-green blotches and silver-white margins) and 'Little Diamond' (small, thin gray-white edges).
Size Trailing or climbing to 1-4 × 1-2 ft (30-120 × 30-60 cm).
Needs Bright light, some full sun; normal to cool room temperature; water sparingly in winter; feed every 2 weeks.

Heptapleurum/Schefflera arboricola 'Hawaiian Elf'
Australian umbrella tree

Features Unbranched stem (bushy if pinched). Green leaves with yellow splashes; each divided into seven or more slender leaflets atop long stalk.
Size Up to 6 × 3 ft (180 × 90 cm).
Needs Bright light, some full sun; minimum temperature 61°F (16°C); humid air; water moderately; feed every 2 weeks during active growth.

Iresine herbstii 'Aureo-reticulata'
Beefsteak plant, chicken gizzard

Features Bushy with soft, succulent red stems. Rounded leaves up to 3 in (7.5 cm) long with greenish tinge and broadly traced with yellow along veins.
Size Up to 2 × 1 ft (60 × 30 cm).
Needs Bright light, some full sun; normal room temperature; humid air; keep soil moist (drier in winter); feed every 2 weeks during active growth.

Peperomia caperata 'Variegata'
Emerald-ripple peperomia

Features Heart-shaped, 1-1½ in (2.5-3.5 cm) long, corrugated, rich green leaves with broad white borders, borne on fleshy pinkish stalks. Flowers in white spikes.
Size Up to 8 × 8 in (20 × 20 cm).
Needs Bright but filtered light; normal room temperature; humid air; water carefully (never overwater); apply half-strength liquid fertilizer monthly.

Peperomia magnoliifolia 'Variegata'
Desert privet

Features Robust plant with red stems. Fleshy, oval, glossy dark green leaves, mostly 3 in (7.5 cm) long, marbled and edged with pale green and creamy yellow.
Size Up to 1 × 1 ft (30 × 30 cm); stems flop over and trail with age.
Needs Bright but filtered light; normal room temperature, humid air; water sparingly; apply half-strength liquid fertilizer monthly.

Plectranthus forsteri 'Marginatus'
Swedish ivy

Features Soft stems, squarish in cross section. Hairy, heart-shaped, 2-2½ in (5-6 cm) long, gray-green leaves, creamy white around scalloped edges.
Size Trailing to 2 ft (60 cm).
Needs Bright light, some full sun; normal room temperature (cool in winter); keep soil moist (drier in winter); feed every 2 weeks during active growth.

Scindapsus aureus/Epipremnum aureum 'Marble Queen'
Pothos

Features Angular whitish stems. Heart-shaped, 4-6 in (10-15 cm) long, glossy white to cream leaves, flecked with gray-green.
Size Climbs to 4 ft (1.2 m).
Needs Filtered light but tolerates shade; normal room temperature; humid air; let soil dry out between waterings; feed every 2 weeks.

Senecio macroglossus 'Variegatum'
Variegated Natal ivy

Features Ivylike, midgreen, three- to five-lobed, 2½ in (6 cm) long leaves with cream marginal patches.
Size Climbing or trailing to 3 ft (90 cm), spreads up to 2 ft (60 cm).
Needs Bright light, some full sun; normal room temperature (cooler temperature in winter); keep soil uniformly damp (drier in winter); feed every 2 weeks during active growth.

Stenotaphrum secundatum 'Variegatum'
Buffalo grass

Features Creeping or trailing stems, rooting at the nodes. Pale cream, 3-12 in (7.5-30 cm) long, blunt-tipped grassy leaves, marked with fine green lines.
Size Trailing to 2 ft (60 cm).
Needs Bright light, some full sun; normal room temperature; humid air (mist foliage); keep soil moist (water less in winter); feed monthly.

Syngonium podophyllum 'Imperial White'
Arrowhead vine

Features Arrow-shaped, three- to five-lobed, 6 in (15 cm) long midgreen leaves, marbled at centers with cream. Mature plants climb, producing much larger leaves (best prevented by pinching).
Size Up to 2 × 1½ ft (60 × 45 cm).
Needs Bright but filtered light, tolerates shade; normal room temperature; water moderately; feed every 2 weeks.

Tradescantia species
Wandering Jew

Features Trailing plants with fleshy stems with nodes (often zigzag). Stalkless leaves, 2-4 in (5-10 cm) long. Small white to pinkish flowers at stem tips. Forms are *T. albiflora* 'Albovittata' (white-striped green leaves), *T. cerinthoides* 'Variegata' (same plant has leaves all-green, all-cream, or half-cream and half-green, all tinged pink when grown in sun), and *T. fluminensis* 'Quicksilver' (fast-growing; leaves striped green and white).
Size Trailing to 2 ft (60 cm) or more.
Needs Bright light, some full sun; normal room temperature; humid air (mist often); keep soil moist (water sparingly during dormancy); feed every 2 weeks during active growth.

COLORED FOLIAGE PLANTS

**Fascinating focal points are offered by the many
houseplants with brilliantly colored leaves, often combined
with startling shapes and lavish textures.**

In addition to foliage plants with white, cream, silver, gray, and gold variegations, there are exotic types with brilliantly colored leaves. The crotons *(Codiaeum)*, for example, bear leaves in an extensive range of color combinations, including yellows, greens, oranges, reds, and blacks.

Rex begonias also produce vivid foliage. The large, hairy, corrugated leaves display a kaleidoscope of green, gray, pink, silver, and flaming red, usually arranged in distinct patterns. Calatheas are truly outstanding for

their intricate leaf patterns and rich colors, which vary from species to species. The similar but easier prayer plants *(Maranta)* are even more exotic, with their leaf ribs picked out in dark crimson.

Unfortunately, some multicolored foliage plants demand a lot of attention, as well as much higher temperatures and a higher degree of air moisture than is comfortable for humans.

Fortunately, there are many colored foliage plants that are much less demanding. The flame

nettles *(Coleus)*, which are brilliantly colored, are some of the easiest plants to grow, thriving outdoors in summer and providing new plants from quick-rooting cuttings. The purple-colored setcreaseas, gynuras, wandering Jews, saxifrages, and polka-dot plants are in the same league and present few problems for the indoor gardener.

Plants with colored leaves may lose some of their brilliance if grown in poor light, but they rarely tolerate strong direct sun. The paler ones are especially susceptible to scorching. For the best results, grow them in very bright but indirect or filtered light.

Keep the foliage clean, as dust soon clogs the leaf pores, impairing the plant's health and vigor and reducing the leaves' luster. Wipe tough-textured leaves gently with a moist cloth; use a soft paintbrush for soft, delicate foliage, which bruises very easily.

Feed colored-leaved plants regularly while they are actively growing; starved plants will not develop good foliage color. Select a fertilizer that has trace elements, since the plant uses them to manufacture the pigments that color the leaves.

Some fleshy-leaved houseplants, such as Christmas cheer *(Sedum × rubrotinctum)*, turn a richer color if kept rather dry and warm. In cooler, moist conditions they grow faster but greener.

The following pages review common colored foliage houseplants, giving the height and spread of mature specimens. Unless otherwise noted, watering and feeding instructions apply to periods of active growth. Feeding instructions presume the use of standard liquid or water-soluble houseplant fertilizer.

◄ **Exotic colors** The glossy-leaved crotons display an astonishing range of colors and leaf shapes that make them the focal point in any group arrangement. The statuesque yellow-edged snake plant offers a fine contrast to the crotons' vibrant colors.

Acalypha wilkesiana 'Macafeeana'
Copperleaf

Features Fast-growing shrub. Coppery green leaves mottled copper, red, and purple.
Size 6 × 4 ft (1.8 × 1.2 m), smaller if grown as an annual.
Needs Bright but filtered light; temperature up to 80°F (27°C) — minimum 59°F (15°C); moist air; keep soil evenly moist; feed every 2 weeks. Best raised from cuttings taken in the fall.

Begonia x *rex-cultorum* hybrids
Rex begonia

Features Large, offset, heart-shaped, rough-textured leaves variably marked with red, pink, purple, silver, and green. Insignificant flowers.
Size 1½ × 1½ ft (45 × 45 cm).
Needs Filtered light, no direct sun; normal room temperature; moist air; keep soil evenly moist (water sparingly during winter); feed every 2 weeks.

Caladium x *hortulanum*
Fancy-leaved caladium

Features Large, arrowhead-shaped, paper-thin leaves on long stalks; suffused, veined, or marbled red, pink, or white.
Size 15 × 12 in (38 × 30 cm).
Needs Bright light but no direct sun; temperature 65°-75°F (18°-24°C); constant high humidity; keep soil moist during growing season (withhold water from fall to winter); feed every 2 weeks.

Calathea makoyana
Peacock plant

Features Large oblong leaves held upright on slender stalks. Leaves patterned green on top, patterned with red and purple on undersides.
Size 2 × 1½ ft (60 × 45 cm).
Needs Diffused bright light; temperature 61°-70°F (16°-21°C); mist daily; keep soil constantly moist (let soil dry out between waterings in winter); feed every 2 weeks.

Codiaeum variegatum pictum
Croton

Features Bushy shrub with glossy, leathery leaves. Cultivars available in a range of leaf shapes and colors — blotched, marbled, or veined yellow, orange, red, or purple, usually changing with age.
Size 3 × 2 ft (90 × 60 cm).
Needs Filtered bright light; normal room temperature; high humidity; keep soil uniformly moist (water sparingly in winter); feed every 2 weeks.

Coleus/Solenostemon cultivars
Flame nettle

Features Bushy, with heart-shaped yellow, cream, orange, red, green, or purple leaves, sometimes slender or incised.
Size 2 × 1 ft (60 × 30 cm).
Needs Bright light, some full sun; temperature 61°-70°F (16°-21°C); water well; feed every 2 weeks; pinch flowers. Propagate from cuttings annually.

Cordyline terminalis
Ti plant

Features Palmlike shrub, eventually treelike as lower leaf fans drop away from erect stems. Clusters of long, pointed and lance-shaped deep green leaves, flushed red when young. Variegated types in shades of green, pink, red, purple, and cream.
Size 3 × 2 ft (90 × 60 cm).
Needs Bright light, filtered in summer; minimum room temperature 50°-55°F (10°-13°C); humid air (mist daily during active growth); water freely to keep soil moist (in winter, water only when soil feels dry); feed every 2 weeks. Brown leaf edges indicate lack of humidity.

Dieffenbachia maculata cultivars
Spotted dumbcane

Features Large, arching pale or dark green leaves with white or cream markings. Poisonous.
Size 2 × 1½ ft (60 × 45 cm).
Needs Bright but indirect light (full sun in winter); minimum temperature 61°F (16°C); high humidity; water moderately all year; feed every 2 weeks during active growth.

Dracaena marginata 'Tricolor'
Dracaena

Features Narrow, arching leaves, striped pink-red, cream-yellow, and green. Old leaves fall off, leaving attractive scars where they were attached to stem.
Size 4 ft × 1½ ft (120 × 45 cm).
Needs Bright but filtered light; temperature 65°-75°F (18°-24°C); moist air (mist often); keep soil moist during growth (water moderately in winter).

Fittonia verschaffeltii
Mosaic plant

Features Creeping plant; olive-green leaves with network of carmine-red or pink veins.
Size 6 × 9 in (15 × 23 cm).
Needs Indirect light, brighter in winter; normal room temperature; high humidity; water regularly but sparingly; give weak liquid fertilizer every 2 weeks during active growth. Pinch growing tips regularly. Best grown in a bottle garden or terrarium.

Gynura aurantiaca 'Purple Passion'
Purple velvet plant

Features Twining or trailing plant with rich purple-felted, deep green leaves and stems.
Size 3-5 × 1½-3 ft (90-150 × 45-90 cm).
Needs Bright light, some full sun in winter; normal room temperature; moist air; water moderately (without wetting the leaves); feed every 2 weeks.

Hypoestes phyllostachya
Polka-dot plant

Features Compact and bushy, with small, pointed-oval, olive-green leaves, spotted soft pink (spots often merge).
Size 15 × 15 in (38 × 38 cm).
Needs Bright light; normal room temperature; high humidity; water moderately (sparingly during winter rest); feed every 2 weeks during active growth. Pinch back to encourage dense growth. Propagate from cuttings every few years — older plants tend to become leggy.

Iresine herbstii
Beefsteak plant

Features Fleshy stems and heart-shaped deep red leaves. 'Brilliantissima' has scarlet-veined plum-red leaves.
Size Up to 2 × 1 ft (60 × 30 cm).
Needs Bright light, some full sun; normal room temperature; moist air; water frequently (sparingly during winter); feed every 2 weeks during growth.

Maranta leuconeura
Prayer plant

Features Bushy plant with oval, deep olive-green leaves strongly patterned with pale green midribs and bright red veins; purple undersides. At night, leaves fold up like hands in prayer.
Size 9 × 12 in (23 × 30 cm).

Needs Filtered light, north- or east-facing window; normal room temperature; high humidity (stand pot on moist pebbles and mist with tepid water daily in dry weather). During active growth keep soil moist and feed every 2 weeks; in winter water moderately only when soil feels dry.

Pelargonium 'Mrs. Cox'
Zonal geranium

Features Bushy plant with round, scallop-edged leaves, midgreen at the center with ring "zones" of red, bronze, and yellow; pungent aroma when bruised. Clusters of pale salmon-pink flowers from spring to fall.
Size 15 × 12 in (38 × 30 cm), larger if grown for several years.

Needs Bright light with at least some full sun; normal room temperature, but keep cool in winter (50°F/10°C); water moderately (very sparingly during winter); apply low nitrogen liquid fertilizer every 2 weeks when growing actively. For compact plants, grow every year from cuttings.

Sansevieria trifasciata
Mother-in-law's tongue

Features Leathery sword-shaped leaves, marbled gray-green; edged gold in 'Laurentii.'
Size 3 × 1½ ft (90 × 45 cm).
Needs Prefers bright light but tolerates shade; temperature 61°-80° F (16°-27° C); water moderately; give half-strength liquid fertilizer monthly during active growth.

Saxifraga stolonifera 'Tricolor'
Mother-of-thousands

Features Stemless, with loose rosette of round olive-green leaves edged cream and rose-pink; purple below. Sprays of tiny white flowers. Trailing shoots bear miniature plantlets.
Size 4 × 6 in (10 × 15 cm).
Needs Bright light, some full sun; normal room temperature; moist air; keep soil slightly moist (water sparingly in winter); feed monthly during active growth.

Scindapsus aureus/Epipremnum aureum 'Golden Queen'
Pothos

Features Angular climbing stems with heart-shaped, glossy golden leaves.
Size Climbs to 4 ft (1.2 m).
Needs Bright but indirect light; normal room temperature; moist air; keep soil uniformly moist; feed every 2 weeks. Grow on moss pole or allow to trail.

Sedum x rubrotinctum
Christmas cheer

Features Fleshy egg-shaped leaves on thin stems, branching from the base; green in color, turning crimson or coppery red under hot, dry conditions.
Size 4-6 × 6 in (10-15 × 15 cm).
Needs Full sun; normal room temperature (cool in winter); water moderately (very sparingly in winter); feed monthly in summer with low-nitrogen fertilizer. Best grown in shallow pot of sandy soil.

Setcreasea/Callisia elegans
Purple heart

Features Trailing; lance-shaped, rich violet-purple leaves have soft bloom. Small magenta-pink flowers in leaf axils in summer.
Size 1 × 1 ft (30 × 30 cm).
Needs Bright light, some full sun; normal room temperature; water moderately; use liquid fertilizer monthly during active growth.

Zebrina pendula/Tradescantia zebrina 'Quadricolor'
Wandering Jew

Features Trailing with sparkling leaves, silver striped with green, red, and white; purple beneath.
Size 3 × 1-2 ft (90 × 30-60 cm).
Needs Bright light; normal room temperature; keep soil evenly moist (slightly drier in winter); feed every 2 weeks when growing actively.

CLIMBERS AND TRAILERS

A wide range of perennial and shrubby foliage houseplants are ideal as screens, wall decorations, and foils for flowering plants.

Exotic but undemanding in their cultural needs, climbing and trailing foliage plants can be invaluable as green or variegated background color, as quick-growing screens and room dividers, or for trailing over the edges of tables or hanging baskets.

Many climbing plants, notably the ivies, are as happy trailing as clambering. True trailing species, however, such as the wandering Jews, with their brittle stems, will not climb upward.

Very few climbing houseplants are self-supporting; most need a support around which they can scramble or twine. As climbing stems grow either clockwise or counterclockwise, they cannot be forced to twine in the direction opposite to their natural habit. If the inclination of a young plant is not obvious, tie its stem loosely to its support until it indicates which way it is going to climb. Various support systems are available from garden centers, or you can make your own.

❑ Thin bamboo or wooden stakes are simple and inexpensive ways of supporting these plants. Used with string ties, they offer good support for individual upright stems. But too many stakes in one pot can look unsightly.

❑ Spiral supports can be bought or made. Drill small holes at intervals through a length of bamboo cane or a ¼-½ in (6-12 mm) diameter hardwood dowel. Then feed stiff nylon cord through the holes and in a spiral up the cane, leaving several open loops. The stems will wind through the loops.

❑ Wire hoops, generally about 1 ft (30 cm) in diameter, are suitable for training small twining plants in a circular fashion to limit their upward growth. They are ideal for flowering climbers such as stephanotis and jasmine.

❑ Plastic indoor trellises come in sections and in many sizes. To install, push the bottom of the trellis into the soil. Usually green, white, or brown, a plastic trellis offers good support for small multistemmed climbers but may not look very natural.

❑ Wooden trellises or special wooden frameworks can be built in any size to support tall, heavy climbers. These supports should be attached to a wall or other rigid surface — not to the pot. The wood can be preserved with a nontoxic stain.

❑ Plastic netting can be fixed between two or more canes or stakes in a large pot. Like a trellis, this is ideal for multistemmed climbers. It can be cut to any desired height and width. Black or dark green netting becomes almost invisible as the climbing plant weaves through it.

❑ Moss-covered poles are ideal for supporting plants with aerial roots — ivies, monsteras, pothos, and some philodendrons. They provide anchorage and moisture, simulating the tree trunk the plant would climb in nature.

Unless otherwise stated, watering and fertilization instructions apply to periods of active growth and presume the use of standard liquid or water-soluble houseplant fertilizers.

▶ **Group display** Climbing foliage plants, including ivies, variegated x *Fatshedera*, and ornamental arrowhead vine, give height to a floor arrangement. A trailing tradescantia fills a gap in the foreground.

Callisia elegans
Purple heart

Features Sprawling plant resembling *Tradescantia*. Pointed-oval, 1-1½ in (2.5-4 cm) long, white-striped olive-green leaves clasping fleshy stems; leaf undersides rich purple.
Size Trails to 2 ft (60 cm); spreads to 1 ft (30 cm).
Needs Bright light with some full sun; normal room temperature; water moderately when in active growth (sparingly during winter rest); feed monthly.

Ceropegia linearis woodii
Rosary vine

Features Slender purple stems cascade from rounded tubers. Small, paired heart-shaped leaves, marbled silver and green on top, purple beneath. Small pink-purple flowers in fall.
Size Trails up to 3 ft (90 cm); spreads up to 10 in (25 cm).
Needs Bright light with some full sun; normal room temperature; water moderately to keep soil slightly moist (drier in winter); feed monthly.

Cissus antarctica
Kangaroo vine

Features Vigorous tendril climber with glossy dark green, pointed-oval leaves up to 4 in (10 cm) long, edged with teeth.
Size Up to 6 × 3 ft (180 × 90 cm).
Needs Tolerates shade, drafts, dry air; normal room temperature; keep soil slightly damp; feed every 2 weeks. Needs support but can be allowed to trail.

Cissus discolor
Rex-begonia vine

Features Vigorous climber with pointed, heart-shaped rich green leaves up to 6 in (15 cm) long, strikingly marbled with silvery white and purple; crimson beneath. The leaf patterning resembles that of rex begonia.
Size Up to 6 × 3 ft (180 × 90 cm).
Needs Bright but filtered light; warm temperature (over 68°F/20°C); humid air; keep soil slightly moist; feed every 2 weeks.

x *Fatshedera lizei* 'Variegata'
Tree ivy

Features Upright climber but can be kept bushy by pinching back or can be allowed to trail. Glossy, white-marked, deep green ivylike leaves up to 8 in (20 cm) wide.
Size 2-6 × 1-4 ft (60-180 × 30-120 cm).
Needs Filtered bright light; normal room temperature (cool in winter); keep soil moist (drier in winter); feed every 2 weeks; support optional.

Ficus pumila
Creeping fig

Features Small branching plant with climbing or trailing stems and tightly packed, oval, dark green leaves up to 1 in (2.5 cm) long.
Size Climbs or trails to 2 ft (60 cm); spreads to 1 ft (30 cm).
Needs Filtered bright or medium light best but tolerates shade; cool to normal room temperature; humid air; water freely (less in fall and winter); feed every 2 weeks; provide support if grown as climber.

Gynura aurantiaca
Purple velvet plant

Features Trailing or climbing stems with toothed rich green leaves up to 6 in (15 cm) long; both have beautifully felted purple hairs, especially when young.
Size Trails or twines to 3-5 ft (90-150 cm); spreads to 3 ft (90 cm).
Needs Bright light, some sun; normal room temperature; humid air; keep soil moist without wetting leaves; feed every 2 weeks; support optional.

Hedera canariensis
Canary ivy

Features Vigorous climber or trailer with rich green, leathery lobed leaves up to 4 in (10 cm) long; marbled gray-green and edged white in 'Gloire de Marengo.'
Size Climbs to 2-4 ft (60-120 cm); spreads 1-2 ft (30-60 cm).
Needs Bright light (some full sun for variegated types); cool to normal room temperature; keep soil slightly damp; feed every 2 weeks; support optional.

Hedera helix
English ivy

Features Vigorous climber or trailer with rich green lobed leaves generally 1-2 in (2.5-5 cm) long. Numerous cultivars with cream, white, or grayish markings.
Size Climbs to 2-10 ft (60-300 cm); spreads 1-2 ft (30-60 cm).
Needs Bright light (all-green types tolerate shade); normal to cool room temperature; keep soil slightly damp; feed monthly; support optional.

Philodendron scandens
Heart-leaf philodendron

Features Climber or trailer with glossy rich green, heart-shaped leaves up to 3-4 in (7.5-10 cm) long; young leaves may be tinted bronze.
Size Generally up to 3 ft (90 cm) tall, spreading to 1 ft (30 cm), but may grow much larger with age.
Needs Bright but filtered light (tolerates semishade); normal room temperature; humid air; keep soil slightly damp; feed every 2 weeks; good on a moss pole.

Piper crocatum
Ornamental pepper

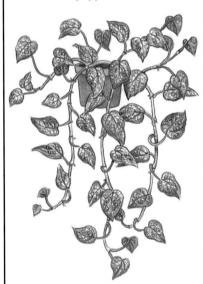

Features Trailing plant with pointed heart-shaped leaves up to 5 in (13 cm) long, colored olive-green with silver and silver-pink markings along the veins; stems and leaf undersides red.
Size Trails up to 7 ft (2.1 m); spreads up to 3 ft (90 cm).
Needs Bright but filtered light; warm room temperature; humid air; keep soil uniformly damp; feed every 2 weeks.

Plectranthus oertendahlii
Swedish ivy

Features Trailing, climbing, somewhat bushy plant packed with almost round, 1 in (2.5 cm) wide, slightly felted leaves, bronze-tinged green and marked with whitish veins and purplish edging.
Size Trails to 3 ft (90 cm) or can be kept bushy by pinching back; spreads to 2 ft (60 cm).
Needs Filtered light, tolerates shade in summer; normal room temperature; good air circulation; water freely during active growth; feed every 2 weeks.

Rhoicissus rhomboidea/Cissus rhombifolia
Grape ivy

Features Tendril climber with slender stems and glossy deep green leaves divided into three 2 in (5 cm) long toothed leaflets.
Size Up to 6-10 × 4-6 ft (1.8-3 × 1.2-1.8 m).
Needs Filtered light, tolerates shade; normal room temperature, cooler (50°F/10°C) in winter; water well; feed every 2 weeks.

Scindapsus aureus/Epipremnum aureum
Pothos

Features Climber or trailer with angular stems, aerial roots, and glossy, leathery, heart-shaped green leaves up to 4-6 in (10-15 cm) long, marbled with yellow.
Size Up to 6 × 1½ ft (180 × 45 cm).
Needs Filtered light, tolerates shade; normal room temperature; keep soil uniformly moist (drier in winter); feed every 2 weeks; good on a moss pole.

Senecio macroglossus 'Variegatum'
Variegated Natal ivy

Features Ivylike trailer or climber with purplish stems and triangular, waxy, midgreen leaves up to 2½ in (6 cm) long, irregularly marked and edged with cream.
Size Trails or climbs up to 3 ft (90 cm); spreads up to 2 ft (60 cm).
Needs Bright light with some full sun; normal room temperature; water moderately (sparingly in winter); feed every 2 weeks; support optional.

Syngonium podophyllum
Arrowhead vine

Features Bushy at first but eventually climbing or trailing. Glossy green, generally arrowhead-shaped leaves up to 8 in (20 cm) long on slender stalks; leaves on young plants may be marked silvery white.
Size Climbs or trails to 6 ft (1.8 m).
Needs Bright but filtered light, tolerates shade; normal room temperature; keep slightly damp; feed every 2 weeks; good on a moss pole.

Tradescantia fluminensis
Wandering Jew

Features Vigorous trailing plant with fleshy stems, prominent leaf nodes, and pointed-oval, stalkless leaves. The cultivar 'Quicksilver' has 3 in (7.5 cm) long leaves, striped green and white.
Size Trails and spreads to 2 ft (60 cm).
Needs Bright light with some full sun; normal room temperature; keep soil slightly damp; feed every 2 weeks.

Zebrina pendula/Tradescantia zebrina
Wandering Jew

Features Vigorous trailing plant whose common name comes from stems' habit of changing direction (wandering) at each node. The cultivar 'Quadricolor' has silvery leaves striped with green, red, and white.
Size Trails up to 3 ft (90 cm); spreads 1-2 ft (30-60 cm).
Needs Bright light; normal room temperature; keep soil slightly damp; feed every 2 weeks.

INDOOR PALMS

Although the elegant palms come mainly from the tropics, they are surprisingly tolerant of less than perfect conditions, poor light, and low temperatures.

In their native habitats, most palms develop a tall, unbranched trunk topped by a crown of fan-shaped or feathery fronds; only a few are low-growing, clustering shrubs. As houseplants, palms tend to grow slowly and never achieve the typical rugged trunk; instead, they produce a few new fronds annually from the crown.

Some types have a single unbranched stem that develops into a short trunk or stumpy base even in container-grown specimens. Other palms are completely stemless or nearly so, forming a cluster of leafstalks. All palms have only one growing point per stem, from which all the leaves develop. If this is damaged or destroyed, it does not regenerate and the whole stem will eventually die. Therefore, although individual leaves may be removed as they yellow, the plants cannot be cut back in any other way.

Palm leaves, or fronds, are either feathery or fan-shaped. Both kinds of leaf are likely to have stalks with a broad, thickened base. The leafstalk itself can be smooth and shiny, hairy, spiny, or toothed at the edges. The stalk of a fan-shaped frond ends at the base of the broad blade. Feathery types produce an extended leafstalk which becomes the midrib of the blade, and the blade is divided into a number of leaflets arranged along the midrib.

In fan-leaf palms, the frond blade spreads out in spraylike fashion from an axis at the tip of the leafstalk. More often than not, the leafstalks of these fronds are spined or toothed at the edges. While indoor palms seldom flower, the smaller palm (*Chamaedorea elegans*) often produces insignificant sprays of yellow ball-shaped blooms on plants 4 or 5 years old. Even when flowers are produced indoors, palms never yield fruit.

Palms are popular plants in large, open vestibules, spacious offices, and hotel foyers, where they seem to thrive on neglect. Certainly, most palms tolerate a wide range of light intensity, hot and dry air, and an erratic watering program. But all will develop into fine plants if given reasonable treatment. Palms prefer airy conditions with some humidity, but they cannot tolerate drafts, extreme heat, or sudden changes in light.

Indoor palms normally have a 2- or 3-month rest period during winter, when watering should be cut back and feeding suspended. Active, though slow, growth begins in midspring and continues until late fall. Most types benefit from standing in a sheltered but bright spot outdoors during the warmer months.

Sizes given on the following pages refer to *height* x *spread* of mature potted plants.

◀ **Elegant palms** Evoking images of grand hotels and Victorian parlors decorated with palms and aspidistras on pedestals, the graceful palms fit just as easily into modern homes. Their undemanding growth habit and elegant foliage allow them to fit into almost any room in the house.

Caryota mitis
Burmese fishtail palm

Features Grayish stalks with fronds that are cut herringbone-style into sections and subdivided into wedge-shaped, folded, ragged leaflets.
Size Up to 8 × 4 ft (2.4 × 1.2 m).
Needs Filtered light; warm temperature (minimum 55°F/13°C); water plentifully but avoid waterlogging; give dilute fertilizer monthly during active growth.

Chamaedorea elegans
Parlor palm

Features Short green trunk with arching fronds; leaflets arranged almost in pairs along a pale leafstalk. Slow-growing plant.
Size Eventually 3 × 3 ft (90 × 90 cm) but generally smaller.
Needs Bright but filtered light; normal room temperature; prefers moist air but tolerant of dry air; water plentifully (moderately in winter); give weak fertilizer monthly during active growth.

Chamaerops humilis
European fan palm

Features Erect fan fronds cut into rigid swordlike segments; stiff, strongly toothed stalks.
Size 3 × 2 ft (90 × 60 cm).
Needs Good light with some direct sun; normal room temperature; water plentifully; feed every 2 weeks during active growth.

Chrysalidocarpus lutescens
Areca palm

Features Glossy and arching light green fronds up to 4 ft (1.2 m) long on tall, deeply furrowed stalks; leaflets arranged in almost opposite pairs.
Size 5 × 4 ft (1.5 × 1.2 m).
Needs Bright but filtered light; minimum room temperature 55°F (13°C); humid air; keep soil moist but avoid sogginess; feed every 2 weeks during active growth with dilute solution.

Cycas revoluta
Sago palm

Features Feathery-looking but stiff, arching fronds rising from pineapple-like, brown-felted water-storing base; needlelike leaflets. Extremely slow-growing cycad — not a true palm.
Size Eventually 4 × 5 ft (1.2 × 1.5 m) but generally much smaller.
Needs Bright light essential; keep room temperature cool in winter (55°F/13°C), warm in summer; tolerates dry air; water moderately; feed monthly except in winter.

Howea belmoreana
Sentry palm, curly palm

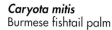

Features Slender plant forming a short trunk with age. Upright to gracefully arching, rich green fanlike fronds, each incised almost to the midrib.
Size Up to 10 × 5 ft (3 × 1.5 m) with age.
Needs Bright light; normal room temperature; tolerates dry air; water plentifully (but avoid sogginess) during active growth (sparingly in winter); feed every 2 weeks only during active growth.

Howea forsteriana
Forster sentry palm

Features Long arching fronds.
Size Up to 10 × 8 ft (3 × 2.4 m).
Needs Tolerates shade and dry
air but prefers bright light; normal
room temperature; water well
(sparingly in winter, mist often); feed
every 2 weeks during active growth.

Licuala spinosa
Queensland fan palm

Features Clustered stems carrying
thorny, slender-stalked fronds
composed of radiating wedge-
shaped leaflets that are ribbed and
end in blunt tips.
Size Eventually up to 4 × 4 ft
(1.2 × 1.2 m) but usually smaller.
Needs Bright but filtered light;
normal to warm room temperature;
humid air; keep soil evenly moist
(less so in winter); feed every
2 weeks during active growth.

Livistona chinensis
Chinese fan palm

Features Generally stemless. Bright
green, glossy, fan-shaped fronds
up to 2 ft (60 cm) wide with deeply
incised edges, drooping at their
tips; toothed stalks.
Size 5 × 5 ft (1.5 × 1.5 m).
Needs Bright but filtered light, no
direct sun; normal room temperature (in winter, will tolerate
45°F/7°C); keep soil evenly moist
(water sparingly in winter); feed
every 2 weeks during active growth.

*Microcoelum
weddellianum/Syagrus cocoides*
Dwarf coconut palm

Features Shiny dark green fronds
with narrow herringbone leaflets
sprout from a short, thickened base;
central rib covered with black scales.
Size Up to 4 × 4 ft (1.2 × 1.2 m).
Needs Filtered light, out of direct
sun; temperature 61°-80°F
(16°-27°C); keep soil damp (drier
in winter); feed monthly during
active growth. Stand pot on tray of
moist pebbles to maintain humidity.

Phoenix canariensis
Canary date palm

Features Stumpy, almost bulbous
stem base. Dark, stiff herringbone
fronds; frond bases covered with
brown fibrous hair.
Size 6 × 5 ft (1.8 × 1.5 m).
Needs Very bright light with some
sun; normal room temperature;
keep soil slightly damp but not wet;
feed every 2 weeks during active
growth. Give winter rest at 50°-
55°F (10°-13°C); water sparingly.

Phoenix roebelenii
Pygmy date palm

Features Thick crown of narrow,
arching dark green fronds covered
with a thin layer of white scales.
Plant may develop more than one
stem.
Size Up to 3 × 4 ft (90 × 120 cm).
Needs Bright light filtered through
translucent curtain; normal room
temperature; keep soil uniformly
damp; feed every 2 weeks during
active growth. Give winter rest
at 50°-55°F (10°-13°C) and water
sparingly.

Rhapis excelsa
Slender lady palm

Features Clustered stems covered with rough brown fiber. Fan-shaped dark green fronds with blunt-tipped segments.
Size Eventually 5 × 5 ft (1.5 × 1.5 m) but generally smaller.
Needs Bright but filtered light; normal room temperature, cool in winter (down to 45°F/7°C); keep soil uniformly damp (but water sparingly in winter); feed monthly during active growth.

Trachycarpus fortunei
Fan palm

Features Slender stem with fan-shaped fronds on finely toothed, long stalks. Young fronds are pleated and covered with fine, light brown hairs. Old main stem covered with coarse brown fiber.
Size Up to 8 × 6 ft (2.4 × 1.8 m).
Needs Very bright light; normal to cool room temperature; keep soil uniformly moist (less so in winter); feed every 2 weeks during active growth.

Washingtonia filifera
Desert fan palm

Features Short, tapered red-brown trunk; long, spiny leafstalks; fan-shaped fronds edged with fine twisted fibers.
Size Up to 5 × 5 ft (1.5 × 1.5 m).
Needs Very bright light; normal to warm room temperature; moist air; water plentifully (moderately in winter); feed every 2 weeks only during active growth.

OTHER INDOOR PALMS

Archontophoenix alexandrae (Alexandra palm) A large palm, suitable for indoors when young. Smooth, short trunk with arching fanlike fronds composed of many narrow leaflets, covered with fine hairs on their undersides, giving a silvery appearance. Plants reach 10 × 7 ft (3 × 2.1 m). Needs bright but filtered light; normal to warm room temperature; plentiful watering and feeding every 2 weeks during active growth.

Caryota urens (Sago or wine palm) Similar to *C. mitis* (Burmese fishtail palm), with drooping fronds composed of many sets of dark green, somewhat leathery leaflets. Leaflets are more triangular in shape and have less jagged edges than those of *C. mitis*; the leaflets are also far less numerous, so that fronds appear looser and more lacelike.

Chamaedorea erumpens (bamboo palm) Clump forming with smooth, slender, upright stems that are knotted at intervals like bamboo. Fronds are arching, deep green, and fanlike. Plants may reach 8 × 4 ft (2.4 × 1.2 m) with age. Cultural requirements as for *C. elegans* (parlor palm), page 76.

Chamaedorea seifrizii (reed palm) Clump forming with slender canelike stems and delicate-looking, lacy, fanlike bluish-green fronds 2-3 ft (60-90 cm) long. Plants reach up to 4 × 4 ft (1.2 × 1.2 m). Cultural requirements are similar to those for *C. elegans* (parlor palm); see page 76.

Corypha utan (Gebang sugar palm) Long-stalked fanlike fronds that are deeply incised into as many as 80 narrow leaflets. Plants reach 3-6½ × 3-6½ ft (30-195 × 30-195 cm). Needs bright light; normal to warm room temperature. Keep soil uniformly damp and feed every 2 weeks during active growth.

Jubaea chilensis (Chilean wine palm) Large fanlike fronds with long, narrow grayish-green leaflets; stem base swollen and covered with brown fibers. Plants eventually reach 5 × 5 ft (1.5 × 1.5 m) with age. Prefers humid air, some shade in summer. Water freely spring through fall (keep it drier in winter).

Livistona australis (Australian fan palm) Very similar to *L. chinensis* (Chinese fan palm) but with slightly larger, dark green leaves and striking spiny leafstalks.

Phoenix dactylifera (date palm) Prickly blue-green fronds arching from slender green stem. Similar to *P. canariensis* (Canary date palm), page 76, but grows somewhat faster and is less showy as houseplant.

Rhapis humilis (reed rhapis) Very slender reedlike stems; fanlike fronds divided into 10 to 20 pointed-tipped leaflets of varying widths. Plants reach up to 8 × 6 ft (2.4 × 1.8 m). Cultural requirements as for *R. excelsa* (above).

Syagrus romanzoffianum (queen palm) Tall, elegant palm with large fanlike fronds of narrow, drooping leaflets. Plants may reach 10 × 7 ft (3 × 2.1 m). Needs bright to medium light; normal to warm room temperature. Keep uniformly damp; feed every 2 weeks during active growth.

Thrinax morrisii (Key palm) Rounded heads of fanlike fronds, which are silvery beneath. Plants grow slowly but may grow too large with age. Cultural requirements as for *Licuala spinosa*.

Washingtonia robusta (thread palm) Similar to *W. filifera* (desert fan palm), above, but taller and thinner, grows faster, and has bright green fronds composed of stiffer, less deeply incised fronds.

INDOOR FERNS

**Ferns, the oldest of all plant groups, neither
flower nor set seed. They are attractive indoor plants
valued for their delicate leaf fronds.**

Ferns belong to several different families of plants, but since they have many features in common, they are invariably treated as a single group. Although ferns come from all parts of the world, only those native to the warmest regions will grow well indoors.

Many tropical ferns are epiphytes — in the wild, their roots grow into rotting vegetation and other debris that collects in crevices between tree branches. Other ferns are terrestrial and thrive in the shady, humid atmosphere at the base of trees or anywhere else at ground level where there is humus-rich soil.

The fronds (a fern's "leaves") and the feeding roots grow from rhizomes, which are fleshy stems acting as food stores. Rhizomes usually grow horizontally underground, but those of some ferns, such as *Asplenium* and *Polystichum*, are stemlike and branching.

The rhizomatous stems of a few ferns, including *Davallia* and *Polypodium*, can creep or cling above ground. When the fern is grown in a pot, these rhizomatous stems, which are often furry, overhang the rim gracefully.

Fronds, a combination of stalk and leaflike blade, vary greatly in size and shape. In outline the blade may be simple and straplike, as in *Asplenium scolopendrium*; divided and feathery, as in *Davallia*; triangular, as in *Adiantum*; or broad and antlerlike, as in *Platycerium*.

The segments of a divided blade are called pinnae. When these pinnae are divided further, the segments are known as pinnules.

Ferns do not flower. Instead, they reproduce by means of dust-like spores borne in brownish cases — called sori — on the undersides of the fronds. Ferns don't require direct sun or even very bright light and, in fact, do well where other houseplants may fail. They are, however, sensitive to overfertilization and should be fed sparingly.

A popular genus of flowering plant, *Asparagus*, has ferny foliage. The ornamental members of this genus are commonly referred to as ferns, and though they are not, they thrive under similar treatment.

▼ **Indoor fernery** Tolerant of poor light and low temperatures, this fern collection displays contrasting forms and colors. Graceful maidenhair and arching Boston ferns are sheltered under a canopy of feathery asparagus.

Adiantum capillus-veneris
Southern maidenhair

Features Arching fronds on black-ish hairlike stalks with light green fanlike pinnae. Rhizomes grow horizontally just below soil surface.
Size Generally up to 10 × 10 in (25 × 25 cm); in ideal conditions, it may be twice this size.
Needs Filtered bright light but no direct sun; room temperature, minimum 55°F (13°C); moist air. Water moderately, keeping soil slightly moist at all times; don't allow fluctuations between excess moisture and dryness. Stand pots on layer of moist pebbles.
   Acid potting soil is ideal; take care not to overfertilize (feed once in spring and once in summer with half-strength liquid fertilizer).

Adiantum hispidulum
Australian maidenhair

Features Fronds divided into spreading sections, each with rows of small, almost oblong, leathery pinnae; reddish brown at first, maturing to midgreen.
Size Up to 1 × 1 ft (30 × 30 cm).
Needs Similar to *Adiantum capillus-veneris*.

***Asparagus densiflorus* 'Sprengeri'**
Emerald feather, asparagus fern

Features Arching plumes of needlelike branchlets (no leaves).
Size 1 × 1 ft (30 × 30 cm).
Needs Full sun but tolerates bright indirect light; normal room temperature; water freely (less in winter); feed every 2 weeks during active growth.

Asparagus falcatus
Sickle thorn asparagus fern

Features Climbing stems with clusters of 2 in (5 cm) long, needlelike green branchlets.
Size To 12 × 1 ft (360 × 30 cm).
Needs Very bright light, no direct sun; normal room temperature; water freely (less in winter); feed every 2 weeks during active growth.

***Asparagus densiflorus* 'Myers'**
Foxtail asparagus fern

Features Soft, upright to arching foxtaillike plumes of bright green, tightly clustered needle-shaped branchlets.
Size Up to 2 × 2 ft (60 × 60 cm).
Needs Very bright light, no direct sun; normal room temperature; water freely (less in winter); feed every 2 weeks during active growth.

Asparagus setaceus
Asparagus fern

Features Wiry stems with flattened sprays of ¼ in (6 mm) long branchlets.
Size Climbs to 10 × 2 ft (300 × 60 cm); 'Nanus' *(shown)* is dwarf.
Needs Very bright light, no direct sun; normal room temperature; water freely (less in winter); feed every 2 weeks during active growth.

Asplenium bulbiferum
Mother spleenwort

Features Lacy midgreen fronds. Small brown bulblets on fronds produce baby ferns.
Size Up to 2 × 3 ft (60 × 90 cm).
Needs Light shade; minimum room temperature 61°F (16°C); keep soil evenly moist (drier in winter); feed half-strength solution monthly during active growth.

Asplenium nidus
Bird's-nest fern

Features Rosette of glossy apple-green, undivided, slightly undulating fronds, each with blackish midrib.
Size Up to 4 × 2 ft (120 × 60 cm).
Needs Moderate light; normal room temperature; water well (less in winter); feed with half-strength solution monthly during active growth.

Asplenium/Phyllitis scolopendrium
Hart's-tongue fern

Features Glossy green, strap-shaped, undivided fronds forming an upright tuft.
Size Up to 2 × 1 ft (60 × 30 cm).
Needs Moderate light; normal room temperature; water moderately (less in winter); apply half-strength liquid fertilizer monthly during active growth.

Blechnum gibbum
Deer fern

Features Glossy green, finely divided fronds in a rosette at top of dark rhizomatous stem, which may become trunklike.
Size Up to 3 × 4 ft (90 × 120 cm).
Needs Bright but filtered light; warm room temperature; moist air; water plentifully; feed with half-strength solution once in spring.

Cyrtomium falcatum
Holly fern

Features Dark green hollylike pinnae, forming stiff, arching fronds.
Size Up to 1½ × 2 ft (45 × 60 cm).
Needs Bright but filtered light; normal room temperature (cooler in winter); water moderately; feed half-strength solution monthly during active growth.

Davallia canariensis
Deer's-foot fern

Features Narrowly triangular, soft-textured midgreen fronds, much divided into tiny pinnae. Creeping scaly rhizomes.
Size Up to 1½ × 1½ ft (45 × 45 cm).
Needs Bright light; normal room temperature; moist air; water well; feed twice annually with half-strength solution.

Nephrolepis exaltata 'Bostoniensis'
Boston fern

Features Long, arching to drooping fronds divided into narrow pinnae. 'Elegantissima' has feathery fronds.
Size Up to 2 × 3 ft (60 × 90 cm).
Needs Bright but filtered light; normal room temperature; water plentifully; feed monthly with half-strength solution during active growth.

Pellaea rotundifolia
Button fern

Features Unusual fern. Arching and spreading fronds with dark green, leathery, buttonlike, ½ in (12 mm) wide pinnae. Borne alternately or almost in pairs on blackish wiry stalks covered with reddish-brown scales. Creeping rhizomes produce spreading clumps of fronds when plant is grown in wide container.
Size Up to 1 × 1 ft (30 × 30 cm).
Needs Medium light; keep from bright sun in summer; mist daily in dry or hot rooms; keep soil moist in growing season (let dry out between waterings in winter); feed every 2 weeks with half-strength solution during active growth. Button fern has shallow roots and is best grown in shallow pot or tray.

Platycerium bifurcatum
Staghorn fern

Features One small sterile frond, replaced yearly, forms a brown papery shield. From the center of this grow larger fertile fronds with antlerlike segments.
Size Up to 3 × 3 ft (90 × 90 cm).
Needs Bright but filtered light; normal room temperature; moist air; water moderately; feed 2-3 times during active growth. Pack rhizomes in sphagnum moss; tie to bark slabs.

Polypodium/Phlebodium aureum
Rabbit's-foot fern

Features Fronds have undulating pinnae. Furry brown rhizomes creep over the soil surface.
Size Up to 3 × 2 ft (90 × 60 cm).
Needs Medium light; normal room temperature; water well (less in winter); apply half-strength liquid fertilizer every 2 weeks during active growth.

Polystichum tsussimense

Features Fronds with slender pinnae and tiny, toothed pinnules.
Size Up to 3 × 2 ft (90 × 60 cm).
Needs Medium to bright light; normal room temperature; high humidity; good air circulation; water plentifully (less in winter); apply dilute fertilizer monthly during active growth.

Pteris cretica 'Albo-lineata'
Cretan brake fern

Features Long-stalked fronds with pinnae in threes. Cream bands mark each side of ribs.
Size Up to 1 × 1½ ft (30 × 45 cm).
Needs Bright but filtered light; normal room temperature; moist air; water plentifully; apply dilute fertilizer monthly during active growth.

Pteris ensiformis 'Victoriae'
Sword brake fern

Features Narrowly triangular fronds have paired pinnae, silvery midribs.
Size Up to 1½ × 1½ ft (45 × 45 cm).
Needs Bright but filtered light; normal room temperature; moist air; water well (less in winter); apply dilute fertilizer monthly during active growth.

Pteris tremula
Australian brake fern

Features Bipinnate feathery fronds with lance-shaped pinnae subdivided into small pinnules.
Size Up to 2 × 1 ft (60 × 30 cm).
Needs Bright but filtered light; normal room temperature; moist air; water well (less in winter); apply dilute fertilizer monthly during active growth.

Selaginella species and cultivars
Spike moss, little club moss

Features Not true ferns but closely related and spore bearing. Mosslike mounded plants or highly branched upright plants with creeping stems. Tiny fleshy leaves in orderly ranks around stems, forming elegant plumes or sprays. Species and cultivars are available with pale green, bright green, golden, or silvery marked green foliage.
Size Generally 2-12 × 6-12 in (5-30 × 15-30 cm).
Needs Medium to low light; warm room temperature; moist air (mist with tepid water often; never use cold water); keep soil moist; apply very dilute liquid fertilizer every 2 weeks during active growth. Ideal plants for a bottle garden.

FLOWERS IN POTS

A wide variety of container plants that produce exotic blooms, brilliant colors, or delicate scents thrive indoors.

Every winter, florists' shops and garden centers are stocked with flowering houseplants — cyclamens, poinsettias, chrysanthemums, azaleas, and primroses — but the range of indoor flowering plants extends far beyond these. Be careful, however, when buying plants sold on windy street corners or in overheated shops or stores; the sudden shock to plants when moved to normal home environments can cause the flowers to drop off and keep new buds from developing.

Most of these are short-term plants, usually discarded after flowering. However, if treated correctly, many can be coaxed into bloom again, especially cyclamens and most azaleas. Poinsettias, too, can be encouraged to flower for a second and even a third year, although the flower bracts, while still brilliant in color, become smaller.

The finest flowering houseplants are those that will reward good care with a more or less continuous display, such as the African violets, Cape primroses, impatiens, and wax begonias. All are easy to grow indoors.

Some of the exotic types, like *Hoya* and *Stephanotis* species, are more exacting in their needs, but their flowering seasons are so spectacular and fragrant that they are worth the trouble.

Certain flowering plants, such as hippeastrums and sinningias, are true herbaceous perennials, retiring into a period of dormancy, when they are best removed to a cool spare room until they begin growing again. The flowers of some houseplants — clivias and aphelandras, for example — provide an additional attraction to handsome foliage. At the other end of the scale are the carefree annuals that flower for months

before coming to a natural end, such as calceolarias, cinerarias, and exacums.

An indoor garden can be bright with flower color at any time of the year. Choose from short-term, long-blooming, and temporary plants, as well as bowls or pots of forced bulbs, to help form a year-round display. As a general rule, flowering plants are less tolerant of poor light and drafts than foliage plants. Temperature fluctuations can result in bud drop, and misting may spoil a flowering plant's delicate petals.

▼ **Unusual containers** Choose containers to suit the mood and style of the decor. Ornate ceramic pots are out of keeping with functional workplaces, but ordinary cans or pails can add a lighthearted touch. Try unconventional containers, such as shells, to mask utilitarian clay or plastic pots.

Achimenes grandiflora
Monkey-faced pansy, nut orchid

Features Bushy deciduous perennial with toothed leaves. Tubular pink-red or purple flowers in summer.
Size 1½ × 1½ ft (45 × 45 cm).
Needs Bright light, out of hot sun; warm temperature and moist soil during active growth (cool and dry when dormant); mist daily during hot spells.

Anthurium scherzeranum
Flamingo flower

Features Dark green lance-shaped leaves. Scarlet spathes with twisted spadix in spring to fall.
Size 1 × 1½ ft (30 × 45 cm).
Needs Partial shade; constant temperature of 61°-70°F (16°-21°C); high humidity (mist often); keep moist and feed every 2 weeks during active growth.

Aphelandra squarrosa 'Louisae'
Zebra plant

Features Dark green leaves with ivory veins. Yellow bracts sprout white flowers, summer to fall.
Size 1¹/₂ × 1 ft (45 × 30 cm).
Needs Bright light; minimum temperature 61°F (16°C); good humidity; water freely and feed every 2 weeks during active growth; let dry out between waterings in winter.

Beloperone guttata/Justicia brandegeana
Shrimp plant

Features Vigorous evergreen shrub with small, lightly hairy leaves. Long, arching flower spikes of pinkish-brown bracts hiding tiny white flowers from spring to fall.
Size 1½-3 × 1-1½ ft (45-90 × 30-45 cm).
Needs Bright but filtered light in summer, direct sun in winter; normal room temperature; good air circulation and humidity. Water moderately and feed every 2 weeks during active growth; water sparingly in winter and keep at constant temperature of 50°F (10°C).

Prune back by up to half in spring to preserve compact shape; take root tip cuttings from prunings. Repot or pot on annually in midspring, using mix of 2 parts standard potting soil and 1 part sphagnum peat. Pinch back growing tips to encourage bushy plants.

Calceolaria hybrids
Slipper flowers, pocketbook flowers

Features Biennials with large, hairy midgreen leaves. Dense clusters of pouched red, orange, or yellow flowers, often blotched with crimson in summer.
Size To 1½ × 1½ ft (45 × 45 cm).
Needs Bright but filtered light; cool temperature (minimum 45°-50°F/7°-10°C); keep soil evenly moist. Discard after flowering.

Campanula isophylla
Italian bellflower

Features Trailing perennial with small heart-shaped leaves. White or blue star-shaped flowers in summer to fall.
Size 6 × 12-18 in (15 × 30-45 cm).
Needs Bright light to full sun; cool temperature (minimum 45°F/7°C); good humidity (mist often); keep evenly moist and feed every 2 weeks during active growth; keep drier in winter.

Clivia miniata

Features Fleshy-rooted perennial with arching, dark green leathery leaves. Large orange-red flower heads in spring to fall.
Size 1½ × 1½ ft (45 × 45 cm).
Needs Bright but filtered light; warm room temperature (winter minimum 50°-55°F/10°-13°C); keep soil moist and feed every 2 weeks during active growth; near-dry in winter.

(minimum 50°-55°F/10°-13°C); increased humidity at high temperatures, no drafts. Water thoroughly when soil feels dry at top. Usually discarded after flowering but can be grown on if cut back hard when foliage dies and rested dry until late spring. Repot and resume watering; flowers produced only if plants given 8 weeks of bud initiation consisting of 14 hours of darkness and 10 hours of light daily.

Features Evergreen shrub with dark green toothed leaves. Short-lived but profuse funnel-shaped crimson, pink, salmon, or yellow flowers in summer.
Size To 6 × 6 ft (1.8 × 1.8 m).
Needs Sunny to very bright light; average room temperature; good humidity; keep soil evenly moist and feed every 2 weeks during active growth; near-dry and cool in winter.

Hippeastrum hybrids
Dutch amaryllises

Features Bulbous, with arching strap-shaped leaves. Large, tall-stemmed white, pink, orange, or scarlet (often bicolored) flower clusters in spring.
Size To 2½ × 1½ ft (75 × 45 cm).
Needs Bright light, full sun; maximum temperature 66°F (19°C); let dry between soakings and feed every 2 weeks during active growth; give dry rest after foliage dies down.

Hoya carnosa
Wax plant

Features Vigorous evergreen climber with oval, fleshy leaves. Scented white to pink flower clusters in midspring to fall.
Size To 10 × 3 ft (300 × 90 cm).
Needs Bright light, some full sun; average room temperature; good humidity; water moderately and feed every 2 weeks during active growth; winter rest at 50°F (10°C). Grow on wire hoops or stakes.

Impatiens wallerana
Impatiens

Features Short-lived mounded perennial with green or bronze leaves. Free-flowering; red, pink, or white (often bicolored) spring to fall.
Size 2 × 1 ft (60 × 30 cm).
Needs Bright but filtered light; minimum temperature 55°F (13°C); good humidity; keep soil evenly moist and feed every 2 weeks during active growth. Pinch back tips for bushiness.

Jasminum polyanthum
Jasmine

Features Climbing shrub with mid-green leaves. Scented, pink-budded white flowers in winter and spring.
Size 3 × 3 ft (90 × 90 cm).
Needs Bright light with several hours of full sun; cool room temperature. Water freely and feed every 2 weeks during active growth; provide support. Cut back after flowering and rest at 39°-55°F (4°-13°C).

Pelargonium 'Aztec'
Martha Washington pelargonium

Features Perennial with lobed and toothed leaves. Clusters of red flowers with white frilly edges in summer.
Size To 24 × 15 in (60 × 38 cm).
Needs Bright light to full sun; temperature 61°-70°F (16°-21°C). Water soil when dry and feed every 2 weeks during active growth. Winter rest at minimum 50°F (10°C); water sparingly; cut stems back by half.

Plumbago auriculata
Cape leadwort

Features Evergreen climber with long, elliptical midgreen leaves. Clusters of pale blue primroselike flowers in spring to fall.
Size 4-6 × 3 ft (120-180 × 90 cm).
Needs Bright light to full sun; room temperature; water freely and feed every 2 weeks during active growth. Winter rest at 50°F (10°C); water sparingly; prune after flowering.

Saintpaulia ionantha
African violet

Features Evergreen plant with hairy, sometimes wrinkled leaf rosettes. Flower clusters in purple, pink, red, white, or bicolored, all year round.
Size 2-8 × 4-16 in (5-20 × 10-40 cm).
Needs Bright, filtered light; minimum temperature 65°F (18°C); high humidity; water from below to keep soil moist; feed monthly.

Senecio/Pericallis x *hybridus*
Cineraria

Features Biennial with heart-shaped, toothed leaves. Daisylike flowers in wide color range in winter and spring.
Size 9-24 × 12-24 in (23-60 × 30-60 cm).
Needs Very bright light to full sun; cool room temperature; set pots on moist pebbles; keep soil moist. Discard after flowering.

Sinningia speciosa
Slipper-flowered gloxinia

Features Tuberous perennial with deep green, purple-backed, veined leaves. Purple bell-shaped flowers in late spring to summer.
Size 8 × 12 in (20 × 30 cm).
Needs Bright but filtered light; normal room temperature; high humidity (mist); keep soil moist and feed every 2 weeks spring to fall; dry soil during winter rest.

Spathiphyllum 'Mauna Loa'

Features Glossy, long-stemmed leaves. Fragrant white flower spathes in spring intermittently to fall.
Size 2 × 2 ft (60 × 60 cm).
Needs Medium, filtered light; normal room temperature; high humidity (mist daily in summer); keep soil moist and feed every 2 weeks during active growth; near-dry winter rest at minimum 55°F (13°C).

Stephanotis floribunda
Madagascar jasmine

Features Slow evergreen climbing shrub with leathery, glossy green leaves. Strongly scented, waxy white flowers from summer to fall.
Size 10 ft (3 m).
Needs Bright but filtered light, normal room temperature; good humidity (mist); keep moist and feed every 2 weeks during active growth; drier in winter. Train on a hoop.

Streptocarpus x *hybridus*
Cape primrose

Features Evergreen perennial of hybrid origin with large, coarse-textured and wrinkled primroselike leaves. Loose clusters of long-stemmed flowers in shades from white to reddish, blue, or violet. Some cultivars offer blossoms with contrasting throats; many can be in flower for 6 months or more.

Size To 12 × 15 in (30 × 38 cm).
Needs Very bright light, out of direct summer sun; normal room temperature (give winter rest at 55°F/13°C). During active growth stand pots on moist pebbles and cover soil with sphagnum moss to keep roots cool. Water freely, allowing soil to dry out somewhat between applications, and feed every 2 weeks; water sparingly in winter.

SCENTED HOUSEPLANTS

**Apart from forced spring bulbs, only a
few indoor plants are scented, but these have
fragrances heady enough to fill a room.**

Most indoor plants are foliage plants that never or only rarely bear flowers because conditions in the home cannot match the tropical climates in which the plants grow naturally. Instead, you can use cut flowers or bowls of potpourri to scent your living room, particularly during winter.

Another popular, if temporary, indoor option is to force spring-flowering bulbs into early bloom. Bunch-flowered narcissi and Dutch hyacinths, for example, are valued for both their flowers and their scent. Gently forced freesias have a delicious perfume, and some frost-sensitive primulas, such as *Primula obconica*,

scent the air with promises of spring. Miniature roses, kept at cool temperatures, have a lingering fragrance, and lily of the valley, potted up and forced at gentle heat, will release a delicious, persistent scent.

Many orchids, with their exotic blooms, are strongly fragrant, notably *Coelogyne, Lycaste,* and several of the easily grown odontoglossums, with their long-lasting flowers.

A few strongly scented species make fine potted plants for the home or can be grown in tubs and open borders in a sunroom or heated greenhouse. They include angel's-trumpet *(Brugmansia),*

wax plant *(Hoya),* Madagascar jasmine *(Stephanotis),* as well as gardenia.

Some of these are easier to grow than others. Gardenias, for example, are so exacting in their cultural needs that they can be difficult to bring to flower in the average living room. *Stephanotis floribunda,* with its heavily scented, waxy white flowers, drops its buds if temperature and humidity fluctuate. The highly fragrant *Jasminum polyanthum* is less temperamental; it covers itself with heady-scented white flowers in spring when grown in a cool room. The *Citrus* species, too, can make accommodating houseplants, and the little calamondin orange (× *Citrofortunella mitis)* is particularly sweet-scented, flowering and fruiting when young.

In all cases, a living room is more likely to be filled with scent if the plants are positioned where there are moving currents of air — but out of cold drafts.

Plants with aromatic leaves, such as certain pelargoniums, release their fragrance only when touched. Stand them where they may be brushed by passersby.

Scented plants benefit from regular feeding with a houseplant fertilizer that is specially formulated for flowering plants — it has the extra potash that flower production calls for. An inexpensive source of potash is the liquid fertilizer sold for tomatoes.

Most scented plants thrive in ordinary potting mix — either loam based or peat based. However, gardenias dislike even the smallest trace of alkalinity and need an acid (ericaceous) potting mix. Water them with rainwater if your tap water is hard (limy).

◀ **Sweet-scented hyacinths** Prized for their densely packed flower spikes, Dutch hyacinths have an unmistakable, almost overpoweringly sweet fragrance. They are specially prepared for early indoor flowering and come in a range of colors — pure white, creamy yellow, pink, red, and blue.

2 weeks during active growth.

Cyclamen persicum
Florist's cyclamen

Features Tuberous-rooted perennial. Butterfly-like red, pink, mauve, or white flowers; small-flowered cultivars have more scent than larger ones. Heart-shaped marbled leaves.
Size Up to 9 × 9 in (23 × 23 cm).
Needs Bright but filtered light; cool temperature; keep soil moist but not soggy; feed every 2 weeks during active growth.

Datura/Brugmansia x candida
Angel's-trumpet

Features Upright shrub. Huge white trumpet flowers up to 10 in (25 cm) long in summer; sweet, heavy scent in evening. Large, midgreen oval leaves.
Size 3-8 ft (90-240 cm) tall.
Needs Bright light to full sun; warm temperature; water generously; feed every 2 weeks during active growth. Cool winter rest.

Exacum affine
German violet, Persian violet

Features Bushy perennial best grown as annual. Small, violet-like, lavender-blue or white, mildly fragrant flowers, summer to early fall. Small, oval olive-green leaves.
Size Up to 1 × 1 ft (30 × 30 cm).
Needs Bright but filtered light; warm temperature; humid air; water plentifully; feed every 2 weeks during active growth; deadhead regularly.

Freesia x hybrida
Freesia

Features Corm-rooted perennial. Arching sprays of funnel-shaped, 1-1½ in (2.5-4 cm) long, very sweetly scented flowers in wide range of colors, including red, pink, mauve, lilac, orange, yellow, cream, and white; flowers often paler in throats and sometimes double.

Upright to arching grasslike leaves up to 9 in (23 cm) long.
Size 1½-2 ft (45-60 cm) tall.
Needs Bright light; cool temperature; water moderately (plentifully when in flower); feed every 2 weeks during active growth. Provide support for floppy stems. After flowering, dry the plants, lift corms, and store in cool, dark, dry place until repotting.

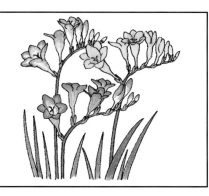

88

Gardenia augusta
Gardenia

Features Evergreen shrub. Double or semidouble, creamy white, strongly sweet-scented flowers in summer and fall, each up to 3 in (7.5 cm) wide; may flower briefly in winter. Lance-shaped, glossy, leathery leaves.
Size 2-4 × 2-4 ft (60-120 × 60-120 cm).

Needs Bright light with some full sun; nighttime temperature no more than 63°F (17°C) when flower buds are forming, normal room temperature at other times; humid air. Keep soil evenly moist (drier in winter) using rainwater if tap water is hard (limy). Feed every 2 weeks during active growth with special acid-based houseplant fertilizer. Deadhead regularly. Use peat-enriched potting mix.

Heliotropium arborescens
Heliotrope, cherry-pie

Features Bushy annual. Fragrant deep violet or white flowers, summer to midfall. Dark green leaves.
Size 1 × 1 ft (30 × 30 cm).
Needs Bright light; cool to normal room temperature; humid air; keep soil moist; feed with weak liquid fertilizer every 10 days during active growth.

Hoya bella/lanceolata bella
Miniature wax plant

Features Arching or trailing shrub. Pendent clusters of sweet-scented, starry, purple-centered white flowers in summer. Lance-shaped leaves.
Size 1 × 1½ ft (30 × 45 cm) or more.
Needs Bright light, some sun; normal room temperature; water moderately; feed every 2 weeks during active growth with high-potash fertilizer.

Hoya carnosa
Wax plant

Features Vigorous climbing shrub. Pendent clusters of powerfully sweet-scented, red-centered, white to pink starlike flowers, mainly in summer (fragrance strongest in evening). Glossy dark green, 2-3 in (5-7.5 cm) long leaves.
Size Climbs to 10 ft (3 m) or can be trained to any size.
Needs Bright light with some full sun; normal room temperature; water moderately; feed every 2 weeks during active growth.

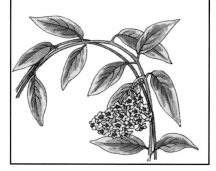

Hyacinthus orientalis **cultivars**
Dutch hyacinths

Features Bulbs. Cylindrical spike of sweet-scented blue, pink, yellow, or white flowers in winter.
Size Up to 12 × 6 in (30 × 15 cm).
Needs Keep dark until leaves are 1 in (2.5 cm) tall, then move into bright light; cool to normal room temperature; keep soil slightly moist.

Jasminum polyanthum
Jasmine

Features Climbing shrub. Sweet-scented, 1 in (2.5 cm) long, pink-budded, white trumpet flowers in winter and spring. Midgreen leaves.
Size May climb to 10 ft (3 m) but can be trained smaller.
Needs Bright light with some full sun; cool temperature; water plentifully; feed every 2 weeks.

Lilium auratum
Golden-rayed lily

Features Bulb. Huge, heavily scented, trumpet-shaped, gold-striped white flowers up to 8 in (20 cm) wide in late summer. Lance-shaped midgreen leaves.
Size Up to 4 ft (1.2 m) tall.
Needs Bright light; cool temperature during early growth, then normal room temperature; water moderately.

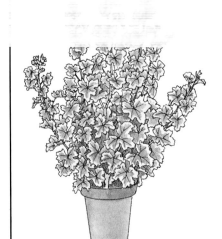

P. capitatum   P. crispum 'Variegatum'   P. graveolens

Features Tough-stemmed bushy perennials. Flowers generally insignificant. Coarse-textured aromatic leaves in many shades of green, sometimes with darker shading or paler variegations, and usually with crimped and incised edges. Scent is released when leaves are touched.

Some species and cultivars suitable for the home include *P. capitatum* (rose scent), 'Cinnamon' (cinnamon scent),

P. crispum 'Variegatum' (lemon scent), *P. x fragrans* (nutmeg scent), *P. graveolens* (rose scent), 'Mabel Grey' (lemon or grapefruit scent), 'Prince of Orange' (orange scent), *P. tomentosum* (peppermint scent).
Size 1½-3 × 1½-2 ft (45-90 × 45-60 cm).
Needs Bright light to full sun; normal room temperature; water moderately; feed every 2 weeks during active growth.

Primula malacoides
Fairy primrose

Features Annual. Tiered clusters of softly fragrant, yellow-centered pink, red, or white ½ in (12 mm) wide flowers in winter and spring. Oval, pale green, slightly hairy, scalloped-edged leaves.
Size To 18 × 10 in (45 × 25 cm).
Needs Bright light with some full sun; cool temperature; keep soil evenly moist; feed every 2 weeks.

Rosa chinensis hybrids
Miniature roses

Features Shrubs. Single, semi-double, or double, ½-1½ in (1.2-4 cm) wide flowers in many colors; some are very fragrant, others less so.
Size Up to 1 × 1 ft (30 × 30 cm).
Needs Bright light, some full sun; normal room temperature (cold in winter); keep soil evenly moist; feed every 2 weeks during active growth.

Stephanotis floribunda
Madagascar jasmine

Features Climbing shrub. Waxy, white, powerfully fragrant trumpet flowers in summer and fall.
Size Climbs to 10 ft (3 m) but can be trained around small hoop.
Needs Bright but filtered light; normal room temperature; humid air, no drafts; during active growth water well and feed every 2 weeks .

bromeliads, the leaves overlap one another to form a watertight types adapt to different conditions if their basic needs are met.

center. This is topped by a bold, usually brightly colored flower head bearing flowers that are about ½ in (12 mm) wide, surrounded by bright and long-lasting bracts. The leaves of this type do not change color during the flowering period, but they are often attractively overlaid with white or silvery scales — a covering that acts as protection during prolonged droughts.

Bromeliad flowers are short-lived, but the bracts remain colorful for several weeks, and they may be followed by berries.

As a rule, each rosette flowers only once, then slowly dies. However, bromeliads usually self-propagate, developing offsets before the main rosette dies. These grow on to replace the old one.

It may take several years for flowers to appear, and nurseries may demand fairly high prices for mature flowering specimens. If you don't mind waiting for results, propagate your own plants from offsets detached when they are about one-quarter the size of the parent plant.

◄ **Tropical jungle effect** Bromeliads, also known as air plants, grow on the floor of tropical rain forests or on tree branches and rock faces. All are rosette forming, often with brilliant leaf colors, marbled horizontal bands or variegated stripes, and a center of dramatic leaf coloring as the flowering season approaches.

Ananas comosus 'Variegatus'
Variegated pineapple

Features Similar to the red pineapple but smaller, with green spiny leaves broadly edged ivory-cream. Leaf edges acquire a rich pink tint if plants are kept in strong light. Plants 6 years old or more may bear a short, stout flower stem with a head of pink or scarlet bracts and bluish flowers. As the flowers fade, a tuft of variegated leaves develops above the flower head. Then, a small inedible pineapple fruit swells below the tuft. (The plant is a variegated and smaller form of the large-fruited edible pineapple.)
Size To 2-3 × 2 ft (60-90 × 60 cm).
Needs Bright light, some full sun; warm temperature; humid air; keep potting mix slightly moist; feed every 2 weeks, year-round.

Billbergia nutans
Queen's tears

Features Lax, narrow, arching olive-green leaves, with reddish tints if grown in sun. Pendent flower spikes with pink, blue-edged petals, backed by long pink bracts.
Size To 1½ × 1 ft (45 × 30 cm).
Needs Bright light, some full sun; normal room temperature; water potting mix moderately; keep rosettes filled; feed as *Aechmea*.

Cryptanthus bivittatus
Earth star

Features Low star-shaped rosettes of undulating leaves colored greenish brown with two lengthwise red or pink stripes. Never flowers indoors.
Size Each up to 3 × 6 in (7.5 × 15 cm), forming larger clump.
Needs Bright light, some full sun; warm temperature; humid air; water sparingly (potting mix only); apply weak foliar fertilizer occasionally.

Cryptanthus bromelioides 'Tricolor'
Rainbow star

Features Irregularly arranged, undulating midgreen leaves with ivory-white edging and striping. Central leaves acquire pink hue in full sun. No flowers indoors. May send out runners with offsets at tips.
Size Up to 9 × 12 in (23 × 30 cm) with age; clump forming.
Needs As *Cryptanthus bivittatus*.

Neoregelia carolinae 'Tricolor'
Blushing bromeliad

Features Glossy midgreen leaves centrally striped with creamy white and tinted rose-pink toward base. As plant matures, whole leaf area becomes suffused with pink; with approach of flowering, central leaves turn brilliant red. Insignificant flower head forms deep in center of leaf rosette.
Size 9 × 18 in (23 × 45 cm).

Needs Bright light with some full sun each day; normal room temperature (minimum 61°F/16°C); humid air (stand pot on saucer filled with moist pebbles, or mist foliage daily); water potting mix moderately, keep rosette filled with fresh soft water or rainwater (tip out and replace water once a month); apply half-strength liquid fertilizer to potting mix and leaves every 2 weeks during active growth, adding some to water in reservoir.

Neoregelia spectabilis
Painted fingernail

Features Leathery olive-green leaves with gray stripes on undersides and tipped at flowering time with 1 in (2.5 cm) long red "fingernails." Blue flowers held in dense circular "nest" of purple-brown bracts deep within leaf rosette.
Size 1 × 2 ft (30 × 60 cm).
Needs As Neoregelia carolinae 'Tricolor.'

Nidularium billbergioides citrinum
Nidularium

Features Bright green fine-toothed leaves. Flower stalk topped with yellow bracts, which conceal white flowers.
Size 10 × 18 in (25 × 45 cm).
Needs Bright but filtered light; normal room temperature (minimum 65°F/18°C); humid air; water potting mix moderately, keep rosette full; apply half-strength liquid fertilizer monthly.

Nidularium fulgens
Blushing bromeliad

Features Arching, spiny-edged pale green leaves, marbled or flecked with darker green. At flowering time rosette center flushes bright cerise. At same time a flower head consisting of dark violet-blue, white-edged flowers and red, green-tipped bracts appears within it.
Size 1 × 1½ ft (30 × 45 cm).
Needs As Nidularium billbergioides citrinum.

Tillandsia lindenii
Blue-flowered torch

Features Narrow gray-green leaves in loose rosette, with purplish undersides. Sturdy flower stalk appearing from center of mature plant carries large fan-shaped head of overlapping rose-pink bracts. White-throated deep blue flowers appear from between bracts one or two at a time in succession throughout summer. *Tillandsia*

cyanea is very similar, with shorter stalk, violet-blue flowers, and rose-red bracts.
Size Up to 20 × 15 in (50 × 38 cm).
Needs Bright, filtered sunlight; cool room temperature in winter (55°F/13°C); humid air (stand pot on saucer of moist pebbles); give half-strength liquid fertilizer monthly. Needs little water at ground level, but mist foliage 2-3 times a week (epiphytic types absorb most of moisture they need through leaf pores).

Tillandsia usneoides
Spanish moss

Features Threadlike trailing stems covered with silver-gray scales (minute scaly leaves).
Size Trails to 3 ft (90 cm) or more with age.
Needs Bright but filtered sunlight; normal room temperature; mist foliage daily. Requires no rooting medium — attach base to twig or bark and suspend plant in high position. Take down and submerge in water once a month; do not feed.

Vriesea fenestralis
Vriesea

Features Arching yellow-green leaves decoratively marked with pale green above and purple below.
Size Up to 2 × 2 ft (60 × 60 cm).
Needs Bright light, some full sun (filtered in summer); normal room temperature at all times; humid air; keep rosette filled with water and moisten potting mix; give soil, foliage, and rosette half-strength liquid fertilizer monthly.

Vriesea splendens
Flaming-sword

Features Dark green leaves with purple-black crossbanding. Tall flower stalk capped with bladelike head of vivid red bracts from which yellow flowers emerge.
Size Up to 2 × 1½ ft (60 × 45 cm).
Needs As *Vriesea fenestralis*.

pears (*Opuntia*) differ in having segmented, flattened stems, or

sun, except for jungle species.

❏ Use a sandy, well-drained soil

globular, viciously spined or smooth leaved, cacti and succulents display a variety of shapes and growth patterns.

Cereus uruguayense 'Monstrosus'
Peruvian apple cactus

Features Distorted mutant form of *C. uruguayense*, having several growing points and covered entirely with irregular, knobbly bumps, forming a grotesque but eye-catching plant. Flowers are rare.
Size Up to 1½ × 1 ft (45 × 30 cm).
Special needs Requires winter rest at 41°F (5°C).

Chamaecereus sylvestri/Echinopsis chamaecereus
Peanut cactus

Features Young shoots resemble peanut shells. These soon lengthen into soft-textured fingerlike stems with areoles of short whitish spines. Scarlet, 1 in (2.5 cm) wide flowers, each lasting about a day, appear in succession for several weeks from early summer. Reliable flowerer.
Size 4 × 6 in (10 × 15 cm) or more.

Cleistocactus strausii
Silver torch

Features Upright, cylindrical stem with about 25 shallow and narrow ribs, completely covered with ¾ in (2cm) long whitish spines, giving an overall silvery coloring. Some spines in each areole are longer — up to 1½ in (4 cm) — and yellowish. Stem may branch at crown to form a clump. Red flowers are borne only on plants more than 10 years old.
Size Each stem up to 4 ft (1.2 m) tall; clumps up to 1 ft (30 cm) wide.

Echinocactus grusonii
Golden barrel cactus

Features Globular plant with 20 or more ribs separated by deep furrows. Stiff golden spines arise in orderly clusters of 8 to 15, each spine being ½ in (12 mm) or more in length, but a few spines in each cluster are twice this length. Yellowish or whitish woolly hairs cluster around base of spines — they are most noticeable at top of plant. Flowers are not produced on small plants indoors, but mature plants may produce 2 in (5 cm) wide yellow flowers in summer. Plant is also known as golden ball cactus.
Size Pot-grown plants rarely exceed 6 in (15 cm) in girth, although plants grown in open ground can reach 1½ ft (45 cm) or more.

Echinocereus pectinatus
Hedgehog cactus

Features Squat cylindrical body, becoming elongated, sometimes branching at ground level to form a clump. About 20 broad but low ribs bear close-set aeroles of short whitish spines. Pink flowers, up to 3 in (7.5 cm) wide, appear in summer, even on quite young plants.
Size Up to 10 × 2½ in (25 × 6 cm).

Echinopsis eyriesii
Sea urchin cactus

Features Globular stem with 11 to 18 narrow ribs, bearing clusters of short brownish spines from grayish cushionlike areoles. Fragrant white flowers, 4 in (10 cm) wide, begin to open at dusk, open fully during the night, and wilt by the next afternoon; they appear during summer.
Size Up to 4 × 4 in (10 × 10 cm).

Epiphyllum 'Ackermannii'/ *Nopalxochia ackermannii*
Orchid cactus

Features Flat, notched, clump-forming stems. Large red flowers, up to 4 in (10 cm) wide, appear in succession all year.
Size Trails to 2 ft (60 cm).
Special needs Jungle cactus. Bright but filtered light. Pot into African violet mix; water plentifully during growth; allow brief rest, with barely moist soil, after each flush of blooms.

Ferocactus latispinus
Devil's tongue, Fishhook cactus

Features Globular stem with spines in clusters of up to 16; most are up to 1 in (2.5 cm) long and whitish, but central ones are up to 1½ in (4 cm) long and red. One spine in each areole is broad and hooked. Violet flowers — but rare indoors.
Size 4 × 4 in (10 × 10 cm), up to 12 × 8 in (30 × 20 cm) with age.

Gymnocalycium mihanovichii
Chin cactus

Features Red-, cream-, or black-stemmed cultivars without chlorophyll are popular. Globular stem with prominent, sharply angled ribs. Red cap and Hibotan cactus (*G. m. friedrichii*) have pink-red stems; 'Black Cap' has black flesh, and there is a creamy form.
Size Up to 6 × 3 in (15 × 7.5 cm).
Special needs Must be top-grafted onto a green rootstock.

Hamatocactus/Thelocactus setispinus
Strawberry cactus

Features Globular stem with notched ribs and 1 in (2.5 cm) long brownish spines — each areole has up to three stouter, hooked spines in the center. Short-lived yellow flowers appear in summer and early fall, followed by red berries.
Size Up to 6 × 4 in (15 × 10 cm).
Special needs Occasionally rinse sticky gum from areoles with warm water.

Lobivia hertrichiana
Cob cactus

Features Globular stem producing many offsets from its base, eventually forming a clump. Each stem produces 11 prominent, deeply notched ribs. Brownish, ½ in (12 mm) long spines in clusters of six to eight with single yellowish central spine up to 1 in (2.5 cm) long.

Scarlet, 2 in (5 cm) wide flowers appear in early summer, several opening at a time but lasting for just a day. However, flowering continues reliably and in succession for a few weeks. Several similar species, cultivars, and hybrids with red or yellow flowers are good indoor plants.
Size Each stem up to 4 × 4 in (10 × 10 cm); clumps to 10 in (25 cm) wide.

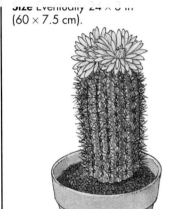

Size Eventually 24 × 3 in
(60 × 7.5 cm).

Features Stems divided into oval,
flattened pads spotted with minute
yellow bristly tufts — glochids — but
no true spines. Pale yellow, 1½ in
(4 cm) wide flowers occasionally
appear on mature plants.
Size Up to 1½ × 1 ft (45 × 30 cm).
Special needs Minimum winter
temperature 50° F (10° C).

Rebutia minuscula
Red-crown cactus

Rhipsalidopsis/Hatiora gaertneri
Easter cactus

Features Flat stems divided into
segments with notched edges. Stems
upright at first, becoming pendent.
Scarlet, 1½ in (4 cm) long flowers
appear in profusion in spring.
Size Trails to 1 ft (30 cm).
Special needs Pot into African violet
mix. Water plentifully when in bud
and flower.

Schlumbergera truncata hybrids
Christmas cacti, Crab cacti

Features Globular stem with many
offsets, covered with rounded
swellings — tubercles — each with
an areole of 20 to 25 short whitish
spines. Red, ¾ in (2 cm) wide flowers
appear in profusion in late spring.
Size Stems up to 2 × 2 in (5 × 5 cm);
clumps up to 6 in (15 cm) wide.

Features Similar
to *Rhipsalidopsis
gaertneri,* but
notched stem edges
are usually more
sharply incised. Profuse
1½-3 in (4-7.5 cm) long
flowers in early winter to midwinter.
Size Trails to 1 ft (30 cm).
Special needs Similar to *R. gaertneri;*
buds drop if plants are moved.

LEAF SUCCULENTS
Many drought-resistant plants, with their fascinating shapes and colors, are ideal for indoor cultivation.

All succulent plants are alike in having an unparalleled ability to store water in their tissues — "succulent" derives from the Latin *sucus,* meaning juice. The water storage tissue is generally concentrated in plump, fleshy leaves (these plants are known as leaf succulents) or in thick, juicy stems (stem succulents).

Stem succulents are often leafless, or nearly so, since the stems of such plants have taken over the food-making process along with water storage. This group encompasses the Cactaceae family (see pages 95–98). Leaf succulents do not bear areoles and usually have thick, smooth leaves, although a few, such as agave, have spine-tipped edges.

Unlike cacti, leaf succulents belong to several different families, which include nonsucculent members. The euphorbias, for example, include some ordinary annual, perennial, and shrubby plants (the poinsettia belongs to the Euphorbiaceae family) as well as spiny succulent species that closely resemble true cacti.

All succulents produce flowers in the wild — they generally originate in dry grasslands or semi-deserts — but many are reluctant to flower in the home. Those that do flower reliably include kalanchoes, echeverias, and crassulas — their colors are often brilliant and the flowers long-lived.

Succulents that don't flower in the home are usually grown for their interesting, often bizarre, shapes or for the attractive coloring of their fleshy leaves. Avoid touching succulents' leaves if they have a grayish or bluish bloom; it rubs off easily.

Although many succulents are easy to grow in the home, others come from such specialized habitats that they are a challenge to even the most experienced grower. One or two succulents, though attractive, are best avoided — for instance, the toad plant *(Stapelia variegata),* with its unusual starry flowers, emits a stench resembling that of rotting garbage.

Most succulents need as much bright light as they can get and thrive in the warmth and low humidity of a sunny room. Pot into a well-drained soil mixture similar to that used for cacti: 1 part coarse sand or perlite and 2 parts standard loam-based potting soil. During active growth, water succulents fairly freely and feed with a high-potassium/low-nitrogen liquid or water-soluble fertilizer, but allow a near-dry, feeding-free rest period.

▲ **Tree succulent** The near-woody stems of *Aeonium arboreum* 'Schwarzkopf' bear fleshy, almost black leaf rosettes.

▼ **Flowering succulents** The winter-flowering *Kalanchoe blossfeldiana* and the jade plant *(Crassula argentea/ovata)* are popular easy-care houseplants.

Features Dense rosettes of fleshy
but hard, whitish-edged gray-green
leaves marked with tubercles.
Orange flowers on 1 ft (30 cm)
stalks in early summer.
Size Up to 6 × 8 in (15 × 20 cm).
Needs Full sun; normal room
temperature (cool in winter); water
plentifully (sparingly in winter); feed
every 2 weeks.

Bryophyllum daigremontianum/ Kalanchoe daigremontiana
Devil's backbone

Features Unbranched stem with
downward-curving blue-green
leaves; inward-curling, saw-toothed
edges carry tiny plantlets.
Size Up to 36 × 6 in (90 × 15 cm)
but unstable once 1 ft (30 cm) tall.
Needs Bright but indirect light;
normal room temperature; water
moderately; feed monthly.

Crassula argentea/ovata
Jade tree, jade plant

Features Trunklike, branching stem
with jade-green fleshy leaves.
Tiny white starry flowers on mature
plants in winter.
Size Up to 3 × 2 ft (90 × 60 cm)
after many years.
Needs Bright light, some full sun;
normal or cool room temperature;
water moderately (sparingly in
winter); feed every 2 weeks.

Crassula muscosa
Rattail crassula

Features Multibranched with
slender, erect stems almost hidden
by minute, pointed, fleshy leaves,
forming four-sided sprays of scaly
appearance — plants also known
as toy cypress crassulas. Insignificant greenish flowers borne in
summer.
Size Up to 8 × 5 in (20 × 13 cm).
Needs As *Crassula argentea/ovata*.

Echeveria derenbergii
Painted lady

Features Cushionlike rosettes of blue-green fleshy leaves with waxy bloom and red tips. Orange-red flowers in spring.
Size Each rosette to 3 × 3 in (7.5 × 7.5 cm), spreading by offsets.
Needs Bright light; normal room temperature (cooler in winter); water sparingly from below; give dilute fertilizer every 2 weeks.

Echeveria harmsii
Red echeveria

Features Branching stems with loose rosettes of lance-shaped, fleshy midgreen leaves, thinly edged with brown and covered with short, soft hair. Scarlet, yellow-mouthed flowers on arching stems appear in late spring and early summer.
Size Up to 1 × 1 ft (30 × 30 cm).
Needs As *Echeveria derenbergii*.

Euphorbia milii
Crown of thorns

Features Dense shrub with thick stems armed with sharp spines. Bright green, nonfleshy, short-lived leaves near growing tips only. Red- or yellow-bracted blooms, any time.
Size Up to 2 × 2 ft (60 × 60 cm).
Needs Full sun; normal room temperature; water moderately; feed every 2 weeks during active growth.

Faucaria tigrina
Tiger's jaw

Features Rosettes of fleshy, gray-green jawlike leaves marked with white dots and edged with softish teeth. Yellow flowers.
Size Up to 4 × 3 in (10 × 7.5 cm).
Needs Bright light with some full sun; normal room temperature (winter rest at 50°F/10°C); water plentifully (sparingly in winter); apply dilute fertilizer monthly.

Gasteria carinata verrucosa
Wart gasteria

Features Paired, fleshy, tapering dark green leaves, covered in gray warts. Leaves arranged in two distinct rows; somewhat concave above and rounded on undersides.
Size Up to 6 × 6 in (15 × 15 cm).
Needs Medium light; normal room temperature (winter rest at 50°F/10°C); water moderately (sparingly in winter); never feed.

Haworthia margaritifera
Pearl plant

Features Cluster-forming rosettes of lance-shaped, tough, dark green fleshy leaves, thickly spotted with pearly white warts.
Size Up to 3 × 6 in (7.5 × 15 cm).
Needs Bright light (no direct sun); high room temperature; water moderately during active growth (sparingly in winter); never feed.

Kalanchoe blossfeldiana hybrids
Kalanchoes

Features Loose rosettes of rich green, sometimes rounded, red-tinted leaves on short stem. Small, four-petaled red, crimson-pink, salmon, orange, or yellow blooms appear in large and compact, domed or flattish, long-lasting clusters from midwinter onward.

Hybrids bought in flower at Christmastime will bloom for 2 to 3 months; then either discard or deadhead and grow on.
Size Up to 1 × 1 ft (30 × 30 cm).
Needs Full sun; normal room temperature; water sparingly; feed every 2 weeks.

Features Sturdy stems carry rosettelike clusters of egg-shaped, pinkish-tinged gray leaves coated with whitish bloom, which is easily rubbed off.
Size Up to 1 × 1 ft (30 × 30 cm).
Needs Full sun; normal room temperature (cooler in winter); water moderately (sparingly in winter); never feed.

Features Tufts of sword-shaped, dark green, marbled and slightly spiraled leaves, edged golden yellow. Tiny insignificant flowers.
Size Up to 3 × 1½ ft (90 × 45 cm).
Needs Bright light but tolerates shade; normal room temperature; water moderately (sparingly in winter); give half-strength fertilizer monthly during active growth.

Sedum morganianum
Donkey's tail

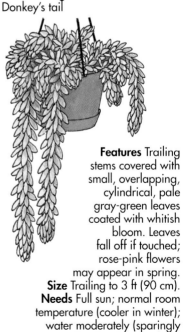

Features Trailing stems covered with small, overlapping, cylindrical, pale gray-green leaves coated with whitish bloom. Leaves fall off if touched; rose-pink flowers may appear in spring.
Size Trailing to 3 ft (90 cm).
Needs Full sun; normal room temperature (cooler in winter); water moderately (sparingly in winter); never feed.

Sedum/Hylotelephium sieboldii
October plant, sedum

Features Nearly circular, slightly toothed gray-green leaves arranged in threes all along trailing stems; leaves centrally blotched creamy white and tinged pink in cultivar 'Medio-variegatum.' Small clusters of pink flowers at stem tips in fall.
Size Trailing to 9 in (23 cm).
Needs As *Sedum morganianum.*

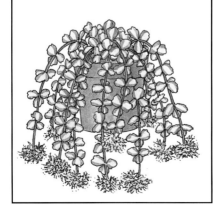

Senecio rowleyanus
String-of-beads

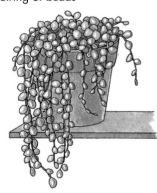

Features Creeping or trailing stems. Beadlike leaves with minute pointed tips. Stems root wherever they touch soil.
Size Stems 2-3 ft (60-90 cm) long.
Needs Bright light with some full sun; normal room temperature (cooler in winter); water moderately (sparingly in winter); feed monthly during active growth.

Decorating with plants

One of the most enjoyable aspects of indoor gardening is arranging your plants to enhance an existing decorating scheme. You can display them singly, place them in groups, allow them to trail from pedestals or wall-mounted baskets, or let them climb around window and door frames.

Windowsills are obvious display areas and are ideal for flowering plants and other light-tolerant species. Decorative containers that harmonize with the color theme of a room can heighten the whole effect. Keep in mind that rows of single pots often look disjointed; group arrangements tend to be much more harmonious. There are numerous ways of arranging plants in groups. Choose all-green foliage plants, for example, for their diverse leaf textures and shapes, and mix them with perhaps one brightly colored plant for contrast. Alternatively, you can relieve the formality of a stiff, upright plant with an arching fern or a trailing plant. In the final analysis, the only restriction is that all the plants in a group arrangement should require similar growing conditions.

There are plants suited to every room in the house, from kitchens to bathrooms, as well as types that will enhance an empty fireplace or a wall niche. Large floor-standing plants are perfect for awkward corners, big hallways, and open landings, or as room dividers and focal points in workrooms and offices. You can also assemble miniature desert cacti gardens, colorful table decorations, and seasonal displays. And there is always the option — not available to the outdoor gardener — of altering a plant arrangement in an instant to suit a change of mood or decorating style.

Windowsill Unobstructed north-facing sites are perfect for flowering plants such as African violets and cyclamens.

many succulents revel in bright light. A south-facing window is ideal, as the summer sun and cooler night temperatures simulate the native habitats of cacti. Sitting in wet soil will cause their roots to rot, so set the cacti's pots on trays of sand that will soak up excess moisture and improve drainage from the soil. When the time for the winter rest approaches, the tray — which here holds a jade plant, a Christmas cheer sedum, a noctocactus, and grafted gymnocalyciums — can be moved to a cooler place.

The variegated *Dracaena sanderana* (bottom center) and pothos (right) enjoy bright light but should be kept out of direct sun.

◀ **Plant stands** Useful for displaying small pots of plants, decorative stands can be positioned in front of a window to give height to regimented rows of plants placed on narrow windowsills. West or even north-facing windows are perfect for plants that prefer good light but won't tolerate scorching sun.

Here, a purple-flowered bush violet (*Browallia speciosa*) and a pink African violet (*Saintpaulia*) colorfully frame the trailing stems of *Ficus pumila*.

course, be moved to a cooler spot when necessary, but west-, east-, and even north-facing windows are more suitable for year-round displays of flowers and foliage. In a Northern winter, however, south windows may be a refuge for light-starved plants.

In winter, windowsill plantings may suffer from cold and drafts, especially at night. Unless the windows are double glazed, it is a good idea to arrange plants on large trays or special plant stands that can be moved to a more protected spot after dark.

Focal points

All too often the overenthusiastic indoor gardener fills every nook and cranny of a room with houseplants, selecting each one according to its individual merits but paying little regard to how they all look together. Usually, the result of such haphazard design is that none of the plants attracts the attention it rightly deserves.

An impressive mature plant should not be a mere accessory, blending in with the furniture,

▶ **Sculptural foliage** A large-leaved banyan tree *(Ficus benghalensis)* of massive proportions makes a stunning focal point next to a winding staircase. Philodendrons, epipremnums, and kangaroo vines *(Cissus)* tumble from the landing, clothing the lofty interior with lush greenery.

▲ Elegant simplicity Matching pedestals topped with rich green arching Boston ferns (*Nephrolepis exaltata* 'Bostoniensis') frame a low settee, creating a feeling of understated elegance.

► Contemporary decor Capable of reaching 10 ft (3 m) indoors, *Dracaena marginata,* with its upright stems and tufts of grassy leaves, complements the clean lines of modern designs.

▼ Matching pairs A classic style demands finishing touches in keeping with the mood. This large window, framed by pleated drapes, is dominated by elegant howea palms.

pedestal chosen to complement the decor of the room. It is well worth the extra expense.

Windows, fireplaces, archways, and open-plan staircases form natural focal points in any room, and their appeal can be enhanced by a few flamboyant plants. But if a room lacks any kind of focal point, create one with a well-placed bold plant. Select a species that has simple but interesting foliage. A multibranched, bushy specimen with a mass of small leaves can look too fussy; an open-structured or irregularly shaped, large-leaved type invariably has greater visual impact.

Room dividers

A large, open room is sometimes used for more than one indoor activity, and it's often a good idea to construct some sort of partition between, for example, a dining area and a sitting area or an office and a kitchen. Several types of screens or curtains are available, but for a more informal, flexible — and decorative —

barrier, an arrangement of climbing, trailing, or bushy plants is the ideal solution.

Choose plants with airy foliage to form a visual backdrop without obstructing the flow of air and light — unless you actually do want to hide one particular part of the room. Dense screens can make a room look small and cast a lot of shade, which is not good for other plants. If large-leaved plants are preferred, space them a good distance apart.

The most natural group of plants to use as dividers are the climbers and trailers. Plant them in floor-standing troughs, individual pots or tubs, or raised containers. Some support is essential and will form the foundation of the screen. Since you may not be able to cover the support completely with foliage, or even want to, make sure the support is attractive in its own right.

Adopt the same principles as for the outdoor support of plants — use trelliswork, wires, netting, or bamboo canes — but bear in

mind that the materials should be more highly finished. With no weather to attack your construction, you should feel free to use top-quality materials.

Room dividers need not stand on the floor; in fact, you may prefer to install rows of hanging baskets or suspended shelving that can hold trailing or bushy plants. These should be hung from pulleys, so that you can tend and water the plants without too much stretching.

The simplest screen is a row of large, bushy potted plants positioned across the floor, perhaps staggered for the best effect. You can also combine any, or all, of the methods described.

▼ **Softening hard edges** Curtains of greenery effectively mask the functional lines and clinical appearance of a high-tech kitchen. Baskets of heart-shaped *Philodendron scandens* and wandering Jew (*Tradescantia albiflora* 'Albovittata') tumble from a shelf suspended from the ceiling.

▶ **Indoor climbers** Ubiquitous but immensely useful in decorating schemes, the grape ivy *(Cissus rhombifolia)* can grow 3 ft (90 cm) in a year. A natural climber equipped with tendrils, it twists its supple stems and green trifoliate leaves around any support. Its companion here, the asparagus fern *(Asparagus setaceus)*, develops a climbing habit when mature; here its bright green fronds lighten the somber grape ivy foliage.

▼ **Room divider** An array of plants strikes a welcoming note and separates the living room from the entrance hall. Weeping figs, ferns, bromeliads, and palms thrive in the filtered light admitted by an overhead skylight.

PLANTS FOR DIVIDERS

Climbers and shrubs
Asparagus fern *(Asparagus setaceus)*
Cape leadwort *(Plumbago auriculata)*
Grape ivy *(Cissus rhombifolia)*
Heart-leaf philodendron
   (Philodendron scandens)
Ivy *(Hedera helix* cultivars*)*
Jasmine *(Jasminum officinale* and
   J. polyanthum)
Swiss-cheese plant *(Monstera
   deliciosa)*
Weeping fig *(Ficus benjamina)*

Trailers
Asparagus densiflorus 'Sprengeri'
Columnea microphylla
Rosary vine *(Ceropegia linearis woodii)*
Spider plant *(Chlorophytum comosum)*
Swedish ivy *(Plectranthus
   oertendahlii)*
Wandering Jew *(Tradescantia
   albiflora, T. fluminensis,* and
   Zebrina pendula)

of plants, the natural light in most domestic living rooms is adequate for growth. Artificial lighting is put to best use, therefore, as a means of enhancing the visual appeal of plants — it can be switched on during the day as well as at night.

Ordinary tungsten filament bulbs, which generate about 70 percent of their energy in the form of heat rather than light, are not suitable for use as the sole source of light for houseplants, since they may scorch the leaves. Fluorescent tubes, preferably 4 ft (1.2 m) long, give excellent light without generating much heat and so are a far better primary light source. Tungsten filament spotlights are useful for dramatic effects, such as backlighting or highlighting, but keep them at least 1½ ft (45 cm) away from the nearest leaf or flower.

Many plants have dramatic outlines and forms in their own right, but with directional lighting the effects can be truly stunning. Look at your plants from all angles and determine what their particular merits are — boldly shaped leaves, delicate filigree foliage, decorative variegations, or

▶ **Lighting effects** The soft light produced by an ordinary lamp can be used to great effect. Diverse foliage shapes are here thrown into silhouette against a wall, making a focal point of a dark corner.

111

amber tones used throughout this spacious living area create an illusion of balmy evenings on a tropical beach. Floor-standing tungsten lights positioned behind treelike figs re-create the relaxing effect of the setting sun.

▲◀ **Mirror images** A clever combination of concealed lighting and floor-to-ceiling mirrors provides an endless array of shadows, highlights, and reflections. The delicate tracery of fern fronds is emphasized by a spotlight beneath the glass table. Similarly, the fresh green foliage of a kangaroo vine, tumbling from a hanging basket suspended on near-invisible nylon cord, is brought to life by a second spotlight. A single low-slung pendent lamp illuminates the glowing flowers of chrysanthemums.

◀ **Fleeting shadows** Domestic light bulbs emit heat that can scorch foliage. Placed at a safe distance, though, the light — while not a substitute for sunlight by day — creates a myriad of delicate shadows on walls and ceilings at night.

shady and in need of brightening.

Luckily, many quite common houseplants originate from deep jungle or forest environments, where light levels are extremely low. These, together with many plants that prefer light but tolerate shade, are ideal for shady parts of the house.

Flowering plants cannot thrive in a dim hallway for long, but there is no reason why certain types should not be moved into poorly lit areas for a short time — chrysanthemums, *Primula obconica*, slipper flower *(Calceolaria crenatiflora),* and *Cyclamen persicum,* for instance. As these like quite cool conditions, they actually prefer to be moved away from a sunny window. But never move a flowering plant just as it is coming into bud; a change in position then often results in bud drop, so wait until several blooms are fully open.

If you do have a bright windowsill in the hallway — perhaps by the front door or along the

green foliage are much more suitable for dark and shady areas

Trailing plants are particularly useful for stairways, where they

▶ **In the shade** Ferns, such as the arching Boston fern, and erect tree ivies (x *Fatshedera*) do well in shady spots or where light is filtered through blinds or sheer curtains. Ivies (*Hedera* species) will tolerate quite deep shade, but variegated types need some light, as here, to maintain their cream-colored leaf margins.

▼ Simple steps A winding staircase makes a suitable platform for foliage plants that prefer subdued light. At the corners of the steps are pots of *Syngonium podophyllum,* sometimes called arrowhead vine because of the shape of its lobed arrowlike leaves. Above them a sickle thorn asparagus fern *(Asparagus falcatus)* receives adequate light, which is reflected through a window onto the whitish wall.

 Asparagus densiflorus 'Sprengeri' trails its dainty, pale green plumes from a window ledge, and a rubber plant *(Ficus elastica)* guards the darker recess at the foot of the stairs.

are free to tumble from hanging containers and window ledges. English ivies *(Hedera helix)* and wandering Jew *(Zebrina pendula)* tolerate low light conditions, but avoid using yellow-leaved and heavily marbled or variegated ivies, which soon turn all-green in poorly lit situations. Asparagus ferns *(Asparagus* species), with their fresh green foliage, and spider plant *(Chlorophytum comosum)* also tolerate poor light conditions and will brighten up the scene.

Smaller, bushy plants are ideal for narrow shelves. Choose from piggyback plant *(Tolmiea menziesii)*, prayer plant *(Maranta leuconeura)*, mosaic plant *(Fittonia verschaffeltii)*, and the smaller ferns, such as trembling bracken

(Pteris tremula) and button fern *(Pellaea rotundifolia)*.

Empty hearths
There is nothing more cosy than a roaring open fire in winter, but for the rest of the year an empty fireplace looks drab. In households where the fireplace is rarely used, the hearth may almost never come to life. In any case, houseplants make wonderful fillers for such areas.

The hearth will not suffer from an occasional spill of water or mind the sticky nectar that drips from flowers. You can even mist moisture lovers daily — with no wallpaper to worry about.

Beautiful rustic containers can be obtained from antique shops — brass coal scuttles, kindling

boxes, and copper cooking pots, for instance. Holders for tongs and pokers can easily double as plant stands. The mantelpiece offers shelving for trailing plants, and taller specimen plants look perfect against the chimney. When the fireplace is serving as a home for plants, close the flue, as cold downdrafts may damage the greenery.

▼ **Fireplace fillers** A deep old-fashioned fireplace is a perfect frame for a summer display of potted plants. Containers of flowering begonias and chrysanthemums add a splash of bright color to the green foliage of spider plant *(Chlorophytum comosum)*, Southern maidenhair fern *(Adiantum capillus-veneris)*, and grape ivy *(Cissus rhombifolia)*.

▼ **Indoor ternery** Most ferns thrive in light shade and moist air. Their graceful fronds make a focal point of an empty hearth.

PLANTS FOR SHADY SPOTS

The following shade-tolerant foliage plants are suitable for bright but not sunny spots and poorly lit areas. Most of the flowering types are best used as temporary fillers, to be replaced as the flowers fade.

Foliage plants
Bird's-nest fern (*Asplenium nidus*)
Boston fern (*Nephrolepis exaltata* 'Bostoniensis')
Burgundy philodendron (*Philodendron* 'Burgundy')
Cast-iron plant (*Aspidistra elatior*)
Dumbcane (*Dieffenbachia maculata*)
Piggyback plant (*Tolmiea menziesii*)
Rex begonia (*Begonia x rex-cultorum*)
Ti plant (*Cordyline terminalis*)

Flowering plants
African violets (*Saintpaulia* hybrids)
Azaleas (*Rhododendron* Indica hybrids)
Begonia Elatior hybrids
Cape primroses (*Streptocarpus* hybrids)
Flamingo flower (*Anthurium scherzeranum*)
Florist's chrysanthemums (*Dendranthema* x *grandiflora* hybrids)
Primula obconica

PLANTS FOR HUMID AIR

Bathrooms and kitchens are often warmer and more humid than living rooms. They are ideal for a variety of foliage plants and herbs.

There is hardly a room in the home that does not benefit from the addition of plant life. Some rooms offer better growing conditions than others in terms of light and temperature — the two most important factors for plant health — but the great majority of indoor plants will grow in less than ideal sites.

When you obtain a new houseplant, determine how tolerant it is by consulting the "Identifying Houseplants" section of this book or by asking a knowledgeable person at a nursery or garden supply center. Then move it from one place to another to discover where it fits in best with the existing decor and where it seems to thrive.

The degree of air moisture, or humidity, can be critical for many tropical foliage plants. But humidity is less of a problem than light and warmth. To increase humidity locally, mist the leaves, stand the pot in a saucer of pebbles kept permanently wet, or set the pot inside a larger pot packed with moist peat. In addition, humidity will increase automatically when plants are arranged in groups rather than displayed as isolated specimens.

In the average house, bathrooms and kitchens often have a higher degree of humidity than living rooms and bedrooms. Such areas can provide good homes for many tropical plants.

Bathrooms

In a traditionally designed house the bathroom is sited against an exterior wall to make for easy plumbing. In this position it usu-ally has at least one window and is reasonably light and airy. The frosted glass often installed in bathroom windows for privacy allows in almost as much light as ordinary window glass, and because it eliminates the need for curtains, the bathroom is often brighter than other rooms. Sun-loving plants thrive on the windowsill, while shade lovers can be put in darker corners — for instance, on the toilet tank, on a shelf over the sink, or suspended in a hanging basket.

Apartment house bathrooms or a second bathroom in larger houses may have no natural light. This makes them unsuitable as permanent homes for plants, but many shade-loving foliage plants can tolerate short periods there — a week or so — provided that bright artificial lighting is switched on for a cou-ple of hours a day. Grape ivy (*Cissus rhombifolia*), philodendron, creeping fig (*Ficus pumila*), and many ferns are suitable.

Temperature and humidity in a bathroom can vary dramatically during each day. At best, the room is warm and often very humid — ideal conditions for most houseplants. At worst, it fluctuates wildly from cold and damp and perhaps drafty to hot and humid. Only the very hardiest of houseplants can cope with such variable conditions.

If you want to grow plants successfully here, keep the bathroom warm in winter and don't open the window to dry out bathtime condensation when outside temperatures are dramatically lower than those indoors. The moisture given off by damp walls, towels, and carpets can, in fact, be beneficial to the plants.

▶ **Steam bath** Most ferns and others with thin, delicate leaves, such as palms, prefer more air moisture than is found in the average living room. The steamy air of a bathroom used for daily showers or baths provides ideal conditions for such plants as umbrella plant (*Cyperus alternifolius*), Southern maidenhair fern (*Adiantum capillus-veneris*), x *Fatshedera lizei*, and African violets (*Saintpaulia*).

When siting plants, remember that the bathroom is a functional area. Don't clutter shelves and sills with plants — they will become a hazard when you need to grab a towel in a hurry. The atmosphere should be one of comfort and luxury. Choose delicately shaped plants or ones with evocative fragrances, such as gardenia, stephanotis, and lemon-scented geranium.

If space is at a premium, opt for slow-growing species that don't need huge pots. Hanging baskets provide a useful means of keeping plants off the work surfaces. And if they are suspended over the bath, there's no need to worry about spilling water.

Select plant containers with care. Heavy ceramic pots can do a lot of damage to tubs and basins if accidentally knocked over. Lighter-weight plastic containers are preferable; these are available in many colors to match any decor. Modern white pots add light to the room; the more traditional clay-colored types often clash with pastel fixtures.

Talcum powder will soon clog leaf pores, so if anyone uses an afterbath powder, clean it off the foliage; spray plants (except those with velvety and hairy leaves) often with tepid water. Avoid using aerosol cans near the plants.

If you intend to set up a display area for plants in a bathroom, never use conventional spotlights to supplement natural daylight — electric lamps must be kept away from splashing water in all bathrooms for safety.

Kitchen plants

A priority in any kitchen, especially where there are children, is safety. Work surfaces should be uncluttered, as pots and pans may have to be moved from the stove quickly without fear of knocking over other items. Try to keep the functional areas — around the cooktop, oven, sink, and dishwasher — free from plants and ornaments.

Instead, reserve a few shelves, a cupboard top, the windowsill, or even the refrigerator top as decorative focal points for plants. You'll discover that houseplants brighten up any kitchen and add a feeling of natural freshness.

There are no hard-and-fast rules about the choice of suitable kitchen plants — it depends on the size of the windows, light levels, and temperature. But plants that favor humid conditions, such as African violets *(Saintpaulia)*, may thrive on a windowsill above a much-used sink and enjoy the extra-moist air.

A windowsill is an ideal spot for propagating small quantities of plants, and you can keep an eye on them regularly. This is also the perfect place for pots of fresh culinary herbs — much more flavorful than dried herbs. Thyme, parsley, bay, lemon balm, rosemary, and chives are easy to grow indoors.

Also welcoming a little extra humidity, many indoor ferns are

▼ **Hanging baskets** *Cissus rhombifolia* and variegated philodendron add a splash of green to a small kitchen without interfering with the work space. Drip saucers attached to the baskets prevent water spillage.

▲ **Kitchen decoration** With some thoughtful planning, even a busy, humid kitchen can have its share of indoor greenery. Baskets of trailing plants and foliage shrubs in corners do not interfere with kitchen activities, and pots of flowering plants make work surfaces more inviting.

◄ **Shelf liners** An out-of-the-way shelf in a well-lit kitchen is ideal for plants that need daily care and prefer a humid environment. It is easy to keep an eye on those that may be in failing health or waiting to be propagated.

▼ **Propagating units** A kitchen windowsill holds a collection of glasses in which avocado pits are being rooted. Cuttings of spider plant (*Chlorophytum*) and *Plectranthus*, as well as impatiens, root easily in jars of water.

excellent in hanging baskets. This type of container has the advantage of keeping plants well above work surfaces. Position them over a sink unit or tabletop so that they are out of the way. When watering a hanging container, never let it drip onto food or into a hot frying pan.

Tall plants can be used effectively as living screens or dividers between an eating area and a cooking and washing area in a large kitchen. A sunny breakfast room cries out for lacy foliage, pretty flowers, and refreshing country fragrances.

Herbs and vegetables

Though they generally produce few or no flowers, many culinary herbs and salad crops are pretty plants in their own right and frequently have an aromatic fragrance when touched. The hardy outdoor types are rarely suitable for year-round cultivation indoors, but they are ideal for short stays on the kitchen windowsill, especially when they are nearly ready for harvesting.

Most herbs and salad crops are garden plants that mature in summer and will not tolerate long spells in the hot, dry air and poor light of an indoor winter. You should cultivate them indoors only in spring through fall, and in the coolest, airiest, and sunniest spot available.

If you want to maintain the most decorative display of herbs possible, choose those from which you pluck just a few leaves, rather than whole shoots; otherwise the plants will soon become bare and unattractive. Marjoram and thyme, for instance, make very good potted plants with their compact, bushy habit, and they actually grow better when given a regular light trim. They will survive in small pots (3-4 in/ 7.5-10 cm) for quite a while, so you should be able to find room for them in even the most cluttered kitchen. Both are strongly flavored, so you need only four to

six leaves at a time for seasoning a dish. The small, half-hardy basil is also an excellent plant for a sunny windowsill.

More vigorous herbs from which you need to pluck several leaves or shoots at once, such as parsley and mint, can also be grown indoors, but they need larger pots — up to 6 in (15 cm) in diameter. These herbs are bushy and will not appear sparse when their leaves are plucked.

As soon as any perennial herb shows sign of stress indoors — yellowing leaves, tall, spindly shoots, or lack of vigor — move it outdoors immediately. Preferably remove it from its pot and plant it in open ground until it fully revives. In subsequent years, divide the plant or take cuttings from it for potting up indoors, keeping a stock in the garden. If you don't have a suitable place in the garden to grow herbs, replace your

kitchen-grown plants with new stock bought from a nursery or grown from seed.

Most salad crops are annuals and, though hardy, may benefit from extra heat and humidity in a northern spring or fall, producing quicker, more tender growth — provided they get enough light and water. Such conditions can be adequately provided on a windowsill indoors, but be prepared to water them at least once a day in summer, often more. Most salad crops can be grown indoors, but avoid crops that go quickly to seed, such as lettuces, when high temperatures are combined with full sun through glass.

The best choices are the fruiting vegetables, such as tomatoes, cucumbers, eggplants, peppers, and chilies. Don't be deterred by the enormous size usually associated with many of these plants — miniature types are available.

▶ **Kitchen herb garden** Pots of herbs fill a kitchen window with aromatic foliage, ready to be plucked when required. Basil and small bay trees are particularly suitable for growing indoors, and germinating seeds also do well on a windowsill. Good light and free air circulation are essential.

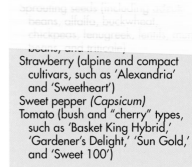

Strawberry (alpine and compact
cultivars, such as 'Alexandria'
and 'Sweetheart')
Sweet pepper (Capsicum)
Tomato (bush and "cherry" types,
such as 'Basket King Hybrid,'
'Gardener's Delight,' 'Sun Gold,'
and 'Sweet 100')

◀▲ **Cooking ingredients** Small pots of
herbs are handy on a windowsill. Parsley,
chives, sage, and lemon balm are content
in small containers, and salad cress takes
up a minimum of space.

◀ **Miniature tomatoes** Cherry tomatoes
are popular, and several varieties can
be grown on a windowsill or even in
hanging baskets. They bear trusses of
sweet-flavored red or yellow fruits, each
about 1 in (2.5 cm) in size.

▼ **Sprouting seeds** Children love to have
their own indoor garden. Salad cress will
sprout in less than 2 weeks, and the tiny
seeds can be sown on a damp paper
towel or in pottery dishes like this one of
a cottage with its own little garden.

only when given support. However, many climbers — notably
ivies, grape ivies, and some philodendrons — are just as happy
trailing as climbing.

be attractive from all sides. Left
to their own devices, trailing
plants will continue to grow
downward, with stems that become much too long and sparsely

window, built as an extension to a living
room, is filled with a range of foliage
plants. Baskets of trailing plants, hung
with fine nylon line, receive maximum
bright light.

bellflower (*Campanula isophylla*) is
an ideal basket plant for a cool, brightly
lit room. Its slender stems are covered
with mauve or white star-shaped flowers
in summer.

RECOMMENDED TRAILERS

It is vital to give a trailing plant the
amount of light it needs. The following list will help you make a match.

Direct sunlight
Emerald feather (*Asparagus
    densiflorus* 'Sprengeri')
Italian bellflower (*Campanula
    isophylla*)
Pothos (*Epipremnum aureum*)
Spider plant (*Chlorophytum
    comosum*)
Wandering Jew (*Tradescantia
    fluminensis*)

Medium light
Columnea (*Columnea microphylla*)
Easter cactus (*Rhipsalidopsis/Hatiora
    gaertneri*)
English ivies (*Hedera helix* cultivars)
Heart-leaf philodendron
    (*Philodendron scandens*)
Impatiens (*Impatiens wallerana*)
Mother-of-thousands (*Saxifraga
    stolonifera*)
Purple velvet plant (*Gynura
    aurantiaca*)
Staghorn fern (*Platycerium
    bifurcatum*)

Shade
Boston fern (*Nephrolepis exaltata*
    'Bostoniensis')
Creeping fig (*Ficus pumila*)
Southern maidenhair fern (*Adiantum
    capillus-veneris*)

enough space underneath for people to pass by. Remember, too, that hot air rises, making the air near the ceiling warmer than the air below. For this reason ivies at ceiling level often shrivel and die.

Trailers, especially those in loam-based potting mixes, can be very heavy, so fasten hooks or brackets firmly to the wall or ceiling. Use lightweight waterproof containers for the larger plants — plastic is better than ceramic for this purpose.

Climbing plants

The common feature of all climbing plants is their inability to grow upright without support. However, this is not necessarily a disadvantage — it makes them just right for clothing walls, pillars, or partitions. Alternatively, many climbers can be left unsupported to trail downward from wall pots, niches, and shelves.

Many plants can be trained to grow both upward and downward around a window or arch. *Philodendron scandens, Cissus rhombifolia,* and ivies, for example, grow upward and sideways with equal success. This can result in some eye-catching arrangements, often giving the impression of a lush garden brought indoors.

The support structure for indoor climbers should be as decorative as possible. Bamboo stakes can be used, but it is better to choose stakes sold specially for indoor use — they are slimmer than normal bamboo and are generally dipped in dark green preservative to improve their appearance and retard decay. For training small container-grown climbers, plastic-coated wire hoops and trellises are also available. For larger plants, use the plastic netting available at most garden centers or a preservative-treated wooden trellis.

Climbers with aerial roots (those appearing from the stems above ground), such as the Swiss-cheese plant, philodendrons, ivies, and epipremnums, all prefer humidity and are suitable for growing against moss stakes.

These are plastic or wooden poles wrapped with moss, which is tied on with nylon line. Keep the moss moist by spraying daily to encourage aerial roots to take a firm hold on the support.

When choosing a support, consider the weight of the plant's foliage and stems. The fleshy leaves and stems of waxflower, philodendron, and Swiss-cheese plant put a lot of strain on a support, so use a sturdy moss stake. Tie in the stems with more nylon line.

Flowering climbers, such as black-eyed Susan vine, passionflower, Cape leadwort, and jasmine, bloom for a few weeks each year, but most indoor climbers are grown for their attractive green or variegated foliage.

▲ **Versatile ivy** The English ivy (*Hedera helix*), available with different leaf shapes and color variegations, is one of the easiest plants to grow. It will climb or trail and tolerates poor light, dry air, and low temperatures.

▶ **Spearhead philodendron** This popular species, *Philodendron domesticum*, is named after its 2 ft (60 cm) long, leathery leaves. In the right cultural conditions, it will slowly climb up to 4 ft (1.2 m) tall when trained on a stake or moss pole.

hoops. It flowers throughout summer and can sometimes be induced to fruit after hand pollination.

◄ **Points of color** The huge size of the vigorous climbing Swiss-cheese plant (*Monstera deliciosa*) is apparent when compared with a 2 ft (60 cm) tall clivia, which has elegantly arching leaf fans and fleshy stems topped with brightly colored flowers.

▼ **Rapid climber** The grape ivy (*Cissus rhombifolia*) can grow 2-3 ft (60-90 cm) in a year. Its sparse, curly tendrils will attach themselves to many surfaces, but ideally the plant should be trained against wire or netting.

RECOMMENDED CLIMBERS

Arrowhead vine (*Syngonium podophyllum*)
Black-eyed Susan vine (*Thunbergia alata*)
Black-gold philodendron (*Philodendron melanochrysum*)
Burgundy philodendron (*Philodendron* 'Burgundy')
Canary ivies (*Hedera canariensis* cultivars)
Cape leadwort (*Plumbago auriculata*)
Emerald feather (*Asparagus densiflorus* 'Sprengeri')
English ivies (*Hedera helix* cultivars)
x *Fatshedera lizei*
Fiddle-leaf philodendron (*Philodendron bipennifolium*)
Golden pothos (*Epipremnum aureum* 'Golden Queen')
Golden trumpet (*Allamanda cathartica*)

Grape ivy (*Cissus rhombifolia*)
Heart-leaf philodendron (*Philodendron scandens*)
Jasmines (*Jasminum mesnyi, J. officinale,* and *J. polyanthum*)
Kangaroo vine (*Cissus antarctica*)
Madagascar jasmine (*Stephanotis floribunda*)
Ornamental peppers (*Piper crocatum* or *P. ornatum*)
Paper flower (*Bougainvillea* x *buttiana* and *B. glabra* cultivars)
Passionflower (*Passiflora caerulea*)
Red-leaf philodendron (*Philodendron erubescens*)
Rex-begonia vine (*Cissus discolor*)
Sickle thorn (*Asparagus falcatus*)
Spearhead philodendron (*Philodendron domesticum*)
Swiss-cheese plant (*Monstera deliciosa*)
Wax plant (*Hoya carnosa*)

SCULPTURAL PLANTS

**Indoor trees and shrubs make spectacular
focal points in the right setting, bringing color
and life to large empty spaces.**

Many popular houseplants are trees or large shrubs in their native habitats. Scaled-down versions of these make impressive specimen plants for large, open living rooms, studios, and workplaces. As their roots are confined in large containers, growth will be slow, but eventually such plants attain a size and beauty that can have as much visual impact in a room as a piece of fine furniture. Don't crowd a room with large plants — one or two well-positioned specimens are more effective than a crowded collection.

Most homes have the odd corner or empty hallway that is too small for a piece of furniture and yet too large to remain empty. A tall plant takes only a little floor space but will fan out above the nearby furniture, creating an arresting sight.

Some garden centers, florists, and houseplant nurseries offer mature specimen plants. But the price is high and the plants may suffer from the move to a new environment. It is usually better to start small and raise your own.

Specimen plants
For focal points in spacious areas, choose perfectly formed plants, ranging from treelike types, such as rubber plant *(Ficus elastica),* weeping fig *(Ficus benjamina),* Swiss-cheese plant *(Monstera deliciosa),* or Norfolk Island pine *(Araucaria heterophylla),* to colorful bromeliads or dracaenas for more modest living rooms.

▼ **Space fillers** The magnificent Swiss-cheese plant *(Monstera deliciosa)* needs plenty of space for its climbing stems and huge, deeply cut leaves, which can grow up to 3 ft (90 cm) long. The more delicate foliage of a dracaena, an araucaria, and ferns provides contrasting shapes and textures.

Swiss-cheese plant, are rapid growers. In their native tropical rain forests they scramble up tall trees, and as houseplants they will reach 15 ft (4.5 m) or more. With adequate support and filtered light, they can be trained up walls and around windows. The weeping fig *(Ficus benjamina)*, on the left, grows more slowly, to 6 ft (1.8 m).

Leaf shapes are often the deciding factor in the choice of specimen plants. Two examples are Spanish bayonet *(Yucca aloifolia),* known for its spiky foliage and statuesque form, and false aralia *(Dizygotheca elegantissima)* with elegant, long-stalked, narrowly divided leaflets. The umbrella tree *(Brassaia actinophylla)* is distinguished by clusters of glossy green leaves radiating from a central point like the spokes of an umbrella. *Philodendron* and *Ficus* species display huge smooth or wrinkled leaves, as much as 3 ft (90 cm) long.

Group arrangements
An effective floor display can also be made with an array of small plants. Choose plants that look good viewed from above, such as bromeliads, which have a rosette leaf arrangement. To simplify day-to-day care and to improve humidity, stand the pots in a tray filled with moist pebbles.

The advantage of group arrangements is that they can be moved around to suit a change of decorative style or to give the plants better light or warmer temperatures during the winter. They can also be augmented with flowering plants for bright color.

Caring for top-heavy plants
Standard loam-based potting mixes are best for tall plants. These mixes are relatively heavy and provide good anchorage for top-heavy plants, which tend to tip over when potted into lightweight, peat-based "soilless" mixes. Watering is also simpler with loam-based mixes. Repotting big specimens is a major undertaking, but it is usually sufficient to replace the top 2-3 in (5-7.5 cm) layer with fresh soil.

As a rule, plastic pots are too light for large plants, so use heavier ceramic containers, if possible. Fiberglass tubs are also fairly stable.

Tall plants in large, heavy containers are difficult to move once positioned. Leave space around the plant to allow for cleaning and general care. And either choose plants that do not grow toward the light and thus will not require turning — small-leaved species and plants with rigid fan-like leaves — or set the containers on trays fitted with casters.

With most shrubby indoor plants, unwanted shoots and dying branches can be removed with a sharp pair of pruning shears. An exception is the Norfolk Island pine, which responds to pruning by dying back and shedding its foliage.

▼ **Lofty interior** A high-ceilinged loft apartment provides a light and spacious environment for a veritable jungle of tropical foliage plants. Treelike brassaias, a massive dracaena, and a willowy weeping fig bring exciting color to this white room.

▲ Yucca tree The exotic-looking yucca is slow-growing. Grown from tree-sections of the same lengths, which sprout roots at one end and rosettes of dark green leaves at the other, it can create a mini-forest when several pieces are potted together.

▶ **Moisture lover** Indoor bamboo plants need plenty of headroom and a deep container filled with moist soil. Boston ferns hide their roots.

SCULPTURAL PLANTS

African hemp (*Sparmannia africana*)
Bamboo (*Arundinaria* species)
Banyan tree (*Ficus benghalensis*)
Canary date palm (*Phoenix canariensis*)
Dracaena fragrans
Dracaena marginata
False aralia (*Dizygotheca elegantissima*)
Japanese fatsia (*Fatsia japonica*)
Kentia palm (*Howea forsterana*)
Norfolk Island pine (*Araucaria heterophylla*)
Parasol plant (*Schefflera arboricola*)
Parlor palm (*Chamaedorea elegans*)
Silk oak (*Grevillea robusta*)
Spathiphyllum hybrids
Spineless yucca (*Yucca elephantipes*)
Umbrella tree (*Brassaia actinophylla*)
Weeping fig (*Ficus benjamina*)

◀ **Weeping fig** With age, the weeping fig (*Ficus benjamina*) develops into a miniature tree with a bare trunk and a head of small glossy leaves. It is tolerant of light shade but enjoys good air moisture.

distasteful. The aroma may be released continuously — especially when the air is warm — as in the culinary thymes, or only when the leaves are bruised or touched.

The scented pelargoniums are a large group, varying in leaf size, flowers, and fragrance. Generally, the flowers are smaller and less flamboyant than those on zonal and ivy-leaved pelargoniums, but their foliage is highly scented. Specialized nurseries offer types with leaves that smell of roses, apples, lemon, or pine, as well as ones with the spicy aromas of nutmeg or peppermint.

Fragrance from aromatic foliage may be strongest when the plants are kept slightly dry. Grow these plants where the leaves will be brushed gently by passersby — in a hallway, for example. Unlike scented flowers, which may be rather transient, aromatic foliage offers year-round delight.

For a combination of beautifully colored flowers and delicate

◄ **Grouped for scent** The Madagascar jasmine *(Stephanotis floribunda)* is noted for the beauty and fragrance of its white flowers. It blooms in summer, at the same time as the little German violet *(Exacum affine)*, which bears delicately scented mauve flowers. The leaves of a lemon-scented pelargonium add a sharp citrus aroma.

▲ **Indoor hyacinths** Popular for forcing, Dutch hyacinths produce thick flower stems topped by 6 in (15 cm) long spikes of densely packed flowers. They are so richly scented that their fragrance can fill an entire room in winter and early spring. These bulbs may be grown in containers full of potting soil or resting just above water in special hyacinth glasses. If grown in water, the bulbs are exhausted at the end of flowering and are best discarded.

▶ **Evening scent** The climbing wax plant (*Hoya carnosa*), with its thick, fleshy leaves, bears clusters of flesh-pink flowers from spring to fall. Their sweet scent is especially strong in the evening, and as the flowers mature, they become sticky with nectar.

Flowering plants
Angel's trumpet (*Datura candida*)
Calamondin orange (× *Citrofortunella mitis*)
Coffee plant (*Coffea arabica*)
Dutch hyacinth (*Hyacinthus orientalis* cultivars)
Florist's cyclamens (*Cyclamen persicum* cultivars)
Gardenia (*Gardenia jasminoides*)
German or Persian violet (*Exacum affine*)
Grape hyacinth (*Muscari armeniacum*)
Heliotrope (*Heliotropium arborescens*)
Jasmines (*Jasminum officinale* and *J. polyanthum*)
Lily of the valley (*Convallaria majalis*)
Miniature roses (*Rosa* cultivars)
Narcissi (*Narcissus poeticus* and bunch-flowered *N. tazetta* cultivars, such as 'Cheerfulness,' 'Cragford,' 'Geranium,' 'Grand Soleil d'Or,' and 'Paper White')
Oleander (*Nerium oleander*)
Madagascar jasmine (*Stephanotis floribunda*)
Wax plants (*Hoya bella* and *H. carnosa*)

Aromatic foliage
Delta maidenhair fern (*Adiantum raddianum* 'Fragrantissimum')
Rosemary (*Rosmarinus officinalis*)
Scented-leaved pelargoniums or geraniums, including *P. crispum* (lemon scent), *P.* × *fragrans* (nutmeg), 'Lady Plymouth' (rose), 'Mabel Grey' (lemon-grapefruit), 'Prince of Orange' (orange), *P. tomentosum* (peppermint)

long-lasting scent, are pretreated and can be brought into flower in roundings. You can repot a plant from a container with an unde- flower (*Browallia speciosa* 'Major') and salmon-pink Elatior begonia.

MULTICOLORED PLANTS

The following popular houseplants are available in different eye-catching colors. You should be able to find at least one to match or contrast with any interior color scheme.

African violets (*Saintpaulia* hybrids)
Azaleas (*Rhododendron simsii* cultivars)
Cape primroses (*Streptocarpus* hybrids)
Chinese hibiscuses (*Hibiscus rosa-sinensis* cultivars)
Cinerarias (*Pericallis* x *hybrida* cultivars)
Elatior begonias (*Begonia* x *hiemalis* hybrids)
Florist's chrysanthemums (*Dendranthema* × *grandiflora* hybrids)
Florist's cyclamen (*Cyclamen persicum*)
Geraniums (*Pelargonium* cultivars)
Gloxinias (*Sinningia speciosa* hybrids)
Impatiens (*Impatiens wallerana*)
Kalanchoe blossfeldiana hybrids
Plumed cockscomb (*Celosia argentea plumosa* cultivars)
Primulas (*Primula malacoides, P. obconica, P. sinensis,* and *P. vulgaris* cultivars)
Slipper flowers (*Calceolaria* × *crenatiflora* cultivars)

Foliage can be equally varied — spiky and imposing or lacy and delicate. Some plants have vividly colored leaves, so you can create a cheerful display year-round.

Ornaments, vases of cut flowers, and everyday household articles can enhance the effect of a living plant display. To achieve more depth, position plants near a large mirror or other reflective surface. As evening falls, the array can be subtly illuminated by a table lamp or spotlight.

Special lamps that can be placed close to plants are available — they don't get as hot as conventional tungsten bulbs and emit a color spectrum more suited to plants. You *can* use ordinary light bulbs, but make sure they're not so close to the plants that they burn the leaves.

Colored foliage
Flowers provide an attractive splash of color in the home, but their season is often limited to a few weeks or even days. For year-round color there's a wonderful choice of plants that display vivid or subtle shades of red, orange, yellow, pink, purple, white, or cream — sometimes all together — on their leaves.

Rich foliage color is often enhanced by surface texture — the wrinkled or corrugated surfaces of rex begonia hybrids are marbled, so the colors actually stand out prominently from the leaf surfaces. In other plants, attractive color effects are increased by intricate leaf shapes and patterns, as well as cut out edges.

The poinsettia *(Euphorbia pulcherrima)* can be considered here, too, since the brilliant red "flowers" are really bracts — modified leaves surrounding the true but insignificant yellow flowers.

Some plants possess both attractive flowers and colorful foliage. For example, the zonal geraniums (actually pelargoniums) include "fancy-leaved" cultivars, of which 'Mrs. Cox' is perhaps the most spectacular; it has salmon-colored flowers above leaves ringed with yellow, copper, red, and green.

Certain plants with colored leaves, especially those with pale ones, scorch much more easily than their green partners, so position them away from direct sunlight. Unlike true variegated leaves (those with white, cream, silver, or gold patches), which lack life-sustaining green chlorophyll pigment in the pale areas, colored foliage is green below the upper surface and so usually tolerates low light levels without reverting to all-green coloring.

▼ **Colorful foliage** The exquisite coloring and delicate texture of caladiums (*Caladium* x *hortulanum*) are maintained only with constant high humidity. The thin arrowhead-shaped leaves, up to 15 in (38 cm) long, come in a range of colors and patterns.

Christmas cheer (*Sedum x rubrotinctum*)
Copperleaf (*Acalypha wilkesiana*)
Mosaic plant (*Fittonia verschaffeltii*)
Polka dot plant (*Hypoestes phyllostachya*)

Purple
Velvet plant (*Gynura aurantiaca* 'Purple Passion')

Yellow/cream
Dumbcanes (*Dieffenbachia maculata* cultivars)
Golden pothos (*Epipremnum aureum* 'Golden Queen')

▲ **Croton** Also known as variegated laurel and botanically as *Codiaeum variegatum pictum*, this superb foliage plant comes in a variety of leaf shapes and colors. The foliage may be strap shaped, oval, or lobed, sometimes with smooth edges and sometimes twisted or wavy. The startling colors appear as speckles or large patches and frequently follow the leaf veins, often nearly obliterating the green background. In contrast, *Calathea ornata* displays its ivory-white stripes in a regular herringbone pattern.

▶ **Flame nettle** Almost as colorful as the croton, flame nettle *(Coleus blumei)* is considerably easier to grow. The coarsely toothed, multicolored leaves come in a variety of shapes; the small blue or white flowers detract from the beauty of the foliage and should be pinched off. Coleus is best grown as an annual but is easily started from cuttings.

COLOR FOR ALL SEASONS

**A host of flowering plants and
indoor bulbs can bring cheerful color to
your home throughout the year.**

Although most houseplants are grown for their foliage, plenty of flowering plants are just as easy to grow, and many will be in flower for most of the year, if given proper growing conditions. The African violets and many *Streptocarpus* hybrids bloom intermittently throughout the seasons.

Many of the spectacular flowering plants sold by florists are, in effect, disposable: they have been bred to produce one beautiful but short-lived display and are best discarded after it ends. Some of these are annuals, such as gloxinias and cinerarias, and will die anyway after flowering. Others are perennials, such as florist's chrysanthemums, but will bloom indoors only when subjected to various kinds of cultural manipulation, which the amateur cannot duplicate.

Some houseplants combine handsome foliage with attractive flowers — for example, the zebra plant *(Aphelandra squarrosa)*. *Clivia* have large fans of dark green strap-shaped leaves and huge heads of attractive flame-colored flowers, which are produced at any time from early spring to late summer.

There are flowering indoor shrubs, climbers, and trailers, in addition to various specialized plant groups, such as cacti, orchids, and bromeliads.

Spring color
Although cyclamens still produce their dainty flowers in spring, the main display is on the wane, and the freshest colors come from the little primulas and winter-flowering pansies. Indoor bulbs, however, are in their prime, either forced for early flowering *(see page 33)* or grown in containers in the open garden and then brought indoors for display as

soon as the flower buds appear.

Bulbs and corms will look their best when planted en masse, outdoors or indoors. They do not have extensive root systems and can be grown successfully in shallow bowls or bulb pans, allowing you to create a miniature blossoming landscape.

Most of the hardy bulbs popular in gardens can be cultivated indoors, though the shorter, more compact species and cultivars do best — others become lanky and

---

▼ **Spring bulbs** The indoor garden comes into bloom while it is still winter outside. Here the early harbingers of spring are sweetly scented hyacinths, trumpet daffodils, tiny blue scillas, and club-shaped grape hyacinths, each potted in vermiculite mulched with sphagnum moss, crushed oyster shells, and charcoal mix and grown in a functional white container.

them outdoors until roots have developed and shoots are clearly visible. Bring them to the flowering stage indoors, in a well-lit spot where the temperature does not exceed 50°F (10°C).

INDOOR BULBS

African corn lilies (*Ixia* cultivars)
Amaryllises (*Hippeastrum* hybrids)
Belladonna lily *(Amaryllis belladonna)*
Blood lily *(Haemanthus)*
Chincherinchee *(Ornithogalum thyrsoides)*
Crocuses (*Crocus* species and hybrids)
Dutch hyacinth *(Hyacinthus orientalis)*
Glory of the snow *(Chionodoxa luciliae)*
Grape hyacinth *(Muscari armeniacum)*
Harlequin flower *(Sparaxis tricolor)*
Ifafa lily *(Cyrtanthus mackenii)*
Irises *(Iris danfordiae* and *I. reticulata)*
Jacobean lily *(Sprekelia formosissima)*
Lily of the valley *(Convallaria majalis)*
Narcissi (*Narcissus* species and hybrids)
Nerine species and cultivars
Scillas (*Scilla* species and hybrids)
Snowdrop *(Galanthus nivalis)*
Spider lily *(Hymenocallis x festalis)*
Spring starflower *(Ipheion uniflorum)*
Triplet lily *(Triteleia laxa)*
Tulips (*Tulipa* species and hybrids)
Winter aconite *(Eranthis hyemalis)*

ungainly when they are grown in the relatively poor light of most indoor environments.

You can plant bulbs in staggered layers in ordinary pots. With narcissi, for instance, place three bulbs on a 2 in (5 cm) layer of potting soil in a 5 in (13 cm) pot, cover their necks with more soil, then set a second layer of bulbs above and between them and repeat until the pot is full.

An attractive display can be created using a glass bowl. Instead of potting soil, use washed pebbles, available in several colors, to support the bulbs. Most bulbs will flower for one season using their own stored food (pebbles provide no nutrients); all they need is water.

Special clay pots, resembling small strawberry pots, can be bought for growing small bulbs in several layers. These pots have holes around the sides, and the bulbs are planted so that the

flowers will grow out through the holes. Crocuses and snowdrops, in particular, look very effective planted in this way.

Hardy bulbs such as narcissi, tulips, crocuses, and hyacinths cannot be forced into bloom successfully indoors 2 years running. Instead, at the end of a single season's bloom, when the flowers have faded and the leaves are beginning to shrivel and die, lift the bulbs and replant them in the garden. They may take a year or so to recover but will eventually flower successfully for many years. Buy fresh bulbs for flowering indoors the following year.

Summer color

The outdoor summer garden traditionally brims with bright flowers, many of them annuals that are discarded after they have finished flowering. In the home the requirements for summer decor are the same — lively colors and

bold shapes. Annuals, such as marigolds, petunias, felicias, and butterfly flowers *(Schizanthus),* can be grown in pots indoors; give them a bright, airy place to keep them from becoming lanky.

For the most successful and continuous display of color indoors, you can grow bushy perennial plants, such as impatiens, begonias, pelargoniums, Cape primroses, fuchsias, and gloxinias. Many come in a vast color range, so you can match them with almost any decor.

As a rule, flowering plants must receive a lot of natural sunlight. Insufficient light, when combined with overwatering,

---

▼ **Summer flowers** The popular and easy-to-grow gloxinias and Elatior hybrid begonias are available in a range of pastel and primary colors. The long-lasting flowers are set off by rich green foliage.

▲ **Summer arrangement** This group of potted plants includes pink- and mauve-flowered *Streptocarpus*, pink and white Madagascar periwinkle (*Catharanthus roseus*), and mauve *Achimenes*. The pink-spotted polka-dot plant provides a good foil.

▼ **Annuals for color** Black-eyed Susan vine (*Thunbergia alata*) will bloom from late spring to fall in a well-lit spot, bearing golden trumpet flowers on climbing or trailing stems. It blends well with the daisy flowers and silvery leaves of anthemis.

Begonia species and hybrids — pink, red, orange, or white

Black-eyed Susan vine (*Thunbergia alata*) — orange or orange-yellow

Bottlebrush (*Callistemon citrinus* 'Splendens') — red

Cape leadwort (*Plumbago auriculata*) — pale blue

Cape primroses (*Streptocarpus* hybrids) — violet, pink, or white

Celosia species — red or yellow flower plumes

Flamingo flower (*Anthurium scherzeranum*) — orange-red

Fuchsia species and hybrids, upright or trailing — purple, red, pink, or white

Geraniums/pelargoniums (*Pelargonium* hybrids) — red, pink, orange, mauve, or white, sometimes bicolored

Gloxinia (*Sinningia speciosa*) — red, purple, pink, or white, often bicolored

Impatiens (*Impatiens* hybrids) — pink, red, orange, or white, often bicolored

Italian bellflower (*Campanula isophylla*) — blue or white

Jacobean lily (*Sprekelia formosissima*) — bronze-red

Madagascar periwinkle (*Catharanthus roseus*) — pink, lavender, or white

Miniature roses (*Rosa* hybrids) — red, pink, yellow, orange, or white, sometimes bicolored

Pachystachys lutea — yellow

Paper flower (*Bougainvillea* x *buttiana* and *B. glabra*) — pink, red, mauve, orange, or white

Yellow sage (*Lantana camara*) — yellow, orange, pink, or red

a refreshing change from the usual shades of orange and red commonly associated with fall. Their marbled leaves blend well with variegated ivies and a pink polka-dot plant.

chrysanthemums can be bought throughout the year, their prominent scent and warm flower colors are reminiscent of the smell of wet soil and the rich tints of falling leaves in autumn.

▲ **Chinese hibiscus** Flowering well into the fall, the Chinese hibiscus *(Hibiscus rosa-sinensis)* begins life as a bushy shrub but, left unpruned, will soon grow to treelike proportions, with a stout main stem and a head of branching side shoots. The large funnel-shaped flowers last for only a day or two, but new buds follow in rapid succession. Red, pink, yellow, orange, and white cultivars are available.

underplanting for bushy fall plants grown in a bowl or box. If you have a "green thumb," try growing a dwarf pomegranate (*Punica granatum* 'Nana'); it may produce a few attractive rose-hiplike fruits on a sunny windowsill in fall.

For a really unusual fall show, the red-hot cattail (*Acalypha hispida*) is also worth a try. It is a large shrubby plant, decked with bright green, slightly hairy leaves and drooping red tassels, which are white in the cultivar 'Alba.'

Winter color

Winter may be the dormant season in the garden, but there is a wide variety of brightly colored flowering plants that can cheer up the home during even the dullest months. Florist's cyclamens as well as indoor azaleas (*Rhododendron* Indica hybrids), in particular, are in abundance everywhere. Although they rarely survive for more than 2 years as houseplants, azaleas are neat, compact shrubs with a wealth of flower clusters available in red, pink, white, orange, and lilac, often bicolored and frequently with ruffled double petals. Win-

ter heaths (*Erica gracilis*), with their massed spikes of dark pink flowers, are also colorful additions to the home; like azaleas, heaths prefer cool conditions and bright light indoors.

The poinsettias (*Euphorbia pulcherrima*) are the most flamboyant of all winter-flowering plants. The tall, vivid red types are more traditional, but some newer cultivars produce bracts in shades of salmon-pink, lime-green, and creamy white, often on more compact dwarf plants.

Bulbs provide some of the brightest colors of all cultivated plants, both in the garden and indoors. Hyacinths, early single and double tulips, narcissi, Dutch crocuses, scillas, dwarf irises, and chionodoxas are the most popular bulbs for planting in bowls from late summer to midfall for winter color.

Most of these bulbs give an extended flowering display if grown in a cool room in a light, airy spot — the dry, overheated conditions common in many homes in wintertime discourage flowering.

Apart from the colorful bulbs, there are several other attractive houseplants — from succulents

like the exotic and colorful kalanchoes to the familiar and popular potted chrysanthemums and cinerarias, which can be grown in a prominent spot in the living room for an instant feeling of summer. The many and varied all-year foliage plants can be grouped with them to create additional color.

Christmas cacti (*Schlumbergera* hybrids), which do not look like cacti at all, are in their full glory during the festive season. Their branches are smothered with deep pink trumpet flowers from midwinter onward.

Cultivated strains of the English primrose (*Primula vulgaris*) have become popular, producing the widest range of flower colors of any winter species — shades of red, pink, orange, yellow, cream, mauve, purple, and white, usually with a yellow eye, are available. Modern strains withstand some forcing and are sold in florists' shops and garden centers from midwinter on. These plants are hardy and ideal for the coolest rooms in the house — a hallway or an attic bedroom. Come spring, plant them out in the garden.

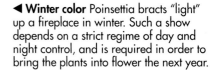

◀ **Winter color** Poinsettia bracts "light" up a fireplace in winter. Such a show depends on a strict regime of day and night control, and is required in order to bring the plants into flower the next year.

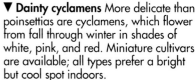

▼ **Dainty cyclamens** More delicate than poinsettias are cyclamens, which flower from fall through winter in shades of white, pink, and red. Miniature cultivars are available; all types prefer a bright but cool spot indoors.

▼ Winter into spring Double-flowered narcissi, such as the orange-centered 'Flower Drift,' can be forced into bloom weeks ahead of those grown outdoors. Like the mottled-leaved Greigii tulips, the bulbs can be planted out in spring.

▲ Temporary color Cinerarias (*Pericallis x hybrida*) bloom annually in late winter. The massive daisylike flowers come in shades of blue, purple, red, pink, and white or combinations of these, all with prominent eyes.

WINTER-FLOWERING PLANTS

Christmas cacti (*Schlumbergera* hybrids)
Cinerarias (*Pericallis x hybrida* cultivars)
Claw cactus (*Schlumbergera truncata*)
Dutch hyacinths (*Hyacinthus orientalis* cultivars — forced bulbs)
Egyptian star cluster (*Pentas lanceolata*)
English primrose cultivars (*Primula vulgaris*)
Fairy primrose (*Primula malacoides*)
False Jerusalem cherry (*Solanum capsicastrum*)
Florist's chrysanthemums (*Dendranthema x grandiflora* cultivars)
Florist's cyclamens (*Cyclamen persicum* cultivars)
German primrose (*Primula obconica*)
Hippeastrum hybrids
Iris danfordiae
Iris reticulata
Jerusalem cherry (*Solanum pseudocapsicum*)
Kalanchoe blossfeldiana
Lily of the valley (*Convallaria majalis* — forced "pips")
Narcissi and daffodils (*Narcissus* cultivars — forced bulbs)
Poinsettias (*Euphorbia pulcherrima* cultivars)
Primula x kewensis
Snowdrop (*Galanthus nivalis*)
Tulips (*Tulipa* cultivars — forced bulbs)

Unusual houseplants

Enthusiastic indoor gardeners may be tempted to grow some rare and unusual plants. Given the right conditions — the correct temperature and humidity are particularly important — a large number of flamboyant plants can be grown successfully in the home. Many orchids are far less demanding than their exotic appearance suggests, and their spectacular blooms last for many weeks. The striking bird-of-paradise can be brought into bloom in most indoor environments with good light, but it does demand ample room and a long winter rest for buds to form.

Bottle gardens and terrariums take up little space and are ideal for those miniature plants that need a higher humidity than can be provided in a living room. Once planted, they need little attention.

Bonsais — miniaturized versions of ancient gnarled trees and shrubs — make superb indoor displays, although they will not thrive if kept continually indoors. Bonsais flourish only when grown outdoors for most of the year, but they may be brought inside for a few weeks at a time to introduce a note of wild beauty into the domestic scene.

Epiphytic "air" plants are relatively easy to grow in the home; they live literally on air alone and make few demands on their owners. In contrast, carnivorous plants are difficult to grow over a prolonged period, but their almost grotesque shapes and voracious appetites can be fascinating.

Jungle effects A richly furnished bay window is a fit setting for flamboyant amaryllises and exotic orchids.

EXOTIC TASTES

**Though they sometimes present a challenge to
the amateur grower, exotic flowering and foliage plants
make striking focal points in any home.**

There is no clear-cut definition of an exotic plant, but any flowering or foliage plant with an aura of mystery and intrigue — especially if it is reminiscent of tropical jungles and forests or of the colorful Far East — could be included.

Many curious plants originate from the humid African tropics, including species and varieties of *Clerodendrum* and *Dracaena*. From drier regions we get *Clivia* and *Strelitzia*, while South Africa is home to exotic bulbs such as *Haemanthus, Lachenalia,* and *Sparaxis*. The warm Asian countries — notably India — supply us with many unusual houseplants, including *Hoya* and *Colocasia*. And South America gives us many unique bromeliads, such as *Billbergia* and *Vriesea*, as well as the arum-related genera *Anthurium* and *Philodendron*.

With other fascinating examples coming from China, Japan, Australasia, the Mediterranean, and Central America, it is obvious that cultural requirements vary widely within this large and diverse group of houseplants. Before buying an exotic plant, make sure that its main requirements for light, temperature, humidity, and water supply can be met in your home. If not, a sunroom or a greenhouse may provide a much better environment.

If you have difficulty in obtaining exotic plants from nurseries or garden centers, consider growing them from seed — many mail-order seed catalogs offer unusual species. Full cultural instructions are usually supplied on the packet. Most exotic seeds require precise conditions for germination, so it is worth buying a small electrically heated propagating unit before you begin.

Humidity — required by many exotic plants — is often difficult to maintain in a home environment. In a greenhouse, hose down the shelves, pots, and floor with water daily during warm weather. This is not a practical solution in the house, so improve humidity by growing several plants in one large container or standing them on a tray filled with moist pebbles; daily misting should be part of routine care. In this way, you will create a humid microclimate around the plants.

▶ **Bird-of-paradise** The striking long-stalked bird-of-paradise *(Strelitzia reginae)*, with its crested orange-and-blue flowers, is rather large for the average living room. Here, it is partnered by orange-flowered *Clivia* and at its base by ivies, ferns, and red *Columnea*. The group needs a space of 4 ft (1.2 m).

▼ Palm house In the controlled temperature and humidity of a greenhouse or sunroom, many foliage plants can begin to approach the size they attain in their natural environments. Palms especially develop typical deeply furrowed trunks and huge arching leaf fans. Here, a hanging basket of trailing ivy-leaved geraniums (*Pelargonium* cultivars) adds vivid color to a veritable jungle of dark green palm fronds.

▲ **Egyptian star cluster** Exotic in name and appearance, the Egyptian star cluster *(Pentas lanceolata)* is quite easy to grow, provided it is given bright light with some full sun. The lavender-pink, magenta, or white flowers appear mainly from late fall to midwinter, though one or two may be produced at any time of year.

▲ ▶ **Gloriosa** A spectacular climber from tropical Africa, the gloriosa lily (*Gloriosa superba* 'Rothschildiana') is best grown in a plant-filled sunroom, where its 6 ft (1.8 m) tall stems can clamber through other plants. The exotic flowers, which resemble Turk's cap lilies, have crimped and wavy crimson petals edged with yellow. They are borne from early to late summer.

▶ **Color harmony** Here, sprays of pink-flowered moth orchid *(Phalaenopsis)*, curious crimson spathes of *Anthurium*, red begonia flowers, and cerise-pink azalea blooms bring color to a collection of foliage plants, including variegated ivies, weeping figs, and calatheas.

Rose grape (*Medinilla magnificana*)
Urn plants (*Aechmea* species)
Wax plant (*Hoya carnosa*)
Yellow sage (*Lantana camara*)

▲ **Bleeding-heart vine** A vigorous twining shrub, the bleeding-heart vine (*Clerodendrum thomsoniae*) makes a stunning feature, with its glossy green foliage and huge sprays of striking red-and-white flowers, from early summer into fall.

It can grow up to 10 ft (3 m) high and is ideal for a greenhouse or sunroom, where the high temperatures and humidity required for flower production can be maintained. In a living room the plant's height can be controlled by regularly pinching the shoot tips during the growing season.

▶ **Terrestrial bromeliads** Growing wild in tropical jungles, the spectacular bromeliads offer many unusual shades of green and gray foliage. The curious flower head consists of a cluster of pointed orange-red bracts, which droop as they open to reveal branched flower stems with upright yellow-and-red flowers.

Another characteristic is the water reservoir contained within the base of the leaf rosette. This must be kept filled at all times, since the roots of most kinds serve as anchors only and do not take up water from the soil.

150

CACTI AND SUCCULENTS

**With their bizarre shapes, varied textures,
and often vivid flowers, cacti and other succulents
are among the most fascinating houseplants.**

Cacti form a large family of prickly succulents — plants that store water in swollen tissues. In common usage, the term "cactus" extends to other succulents as well. But although all cacti are succulents, not all succulents are cacti (those that lack spines are likely to be succulents). Visually, cacti are very different from other plants — they lack typical leaves, have a geometric shape and pattern of spines, and may bear exotic blooms.

From the vast number of cacti available — some easy to grow, others more challenging — you can build a good plant collection. Many are modest in size and tend to look out of proportion in individual pots. For a more appealing array, plant them in groups in a large, shallow container, using gravel, stones, or bark chips to "landscape" the surface.

Most cacti come from deserts and enjoy bright sunlight, so a south- or west-facing window is ideal. However, a few come from tropical forests — *Epiphyllum*, *Hatiora,* and *Schlumbergera,* for instance — and prefer a shady east- or north-facing spot.

Desert cacti need a cool, dry winter rest in order to flower well. In winter they should be kept in a cool room, where the temperature stays between 41°F (5°C) and 50°F (10°C).

In the growing period, water desert cacti whenever the soil looks dry. When dormant they need little water, just enough to

---

▼ **Desert cacti** A group arrangement is the most effective way of displaying the different forms and textures of desert cacti. Most grow slowly and have shallow roots; they thrive in well-drained soil and bright sun.

funnel-shaped flowers of pink, bright red, or yellow.

The stem-grafted *Gymnocalycium mihanovichii* is topped with unusual pink or yellow flowers (foreground).

▼ **Desert garden** A shallow box is transformed into an arid desert landscape of cacti and succulents, including a viciously spiny barrel cactus *(Echinocactus)* in the foreground and a smooth and shiny-leaved jade plant. Gravel covering the potting soil adds to the desertlike effect.

stop the soil from drying out completely. Forest cacti must never dry out, even in winter, but don't overwater them — the roots rot easily. When in flower and during active growth, feed both cacti and succulents with a low-nitrogen high-potassium fertilizer every 2 weeks.

Succulents

The term "cactus" correctly applies only to members of the Cactaceae family; it does not include the aloes, agaves, crassulas, euphorbias, kalanchoes, and many other fleshy-leaved plants. These true succulents have growing regimes that are different from cacti.

In those parts of the world where water is scarce or very seasonal, these plants have evolved the ability to store water, when it *is* available, in swollen stems and leaves. Their leaves and stems are often decorative and always distinctive. Although a few true succulents are spiny — and a few cacti are spineless — they differ from cacti in being without areoles, the tiny swellings from which cactus spines and flower buds emerge.

As houseplants, cacti and other succulents are especially valuable where regular watering cannot be guaranteed — many can survive for several weeks, or even months, without water. However, when they are watered, they prefer to have a good drenching before being left to dry out again. They rot at their base if kept constantly moist.

Some succulents flower reliably indoors; they include *Kalanchoe blossfeldiana* and its hybrids, *Crassula* (previously *Rochea*) *coccinea,* and many echeverias. Others, however, have colorful leaves or swollen stems and are unlikely to flower in the home.

Except for haworthias and gasterias, which will tolerate some shade, all succulent houseplants must be given as much direct sunlight as possible — remember that their native habitat is desert, except for a few forest types that prefer more subdued light. This means that the best spot for a succulent desert plant is in or near a south-facing window. Give plants a quarter turn every so often to prevent them from growing toward the light. A sign of poor light is elongated and floppy growth — especially noticeable with rosette-forming succulents, such as echeverias, which should remain low and compact.

Unlike cacti, which do not flower well unless given a dormant period of cool temperatures in winter, most succulents will thrive in the warm, dry air of the typical heated living room, flowering happily in such conditions. A few types, however, do share cacti's need for a cool winter rest.

Like many houseplants, succulents benefit from being placed outdoors in their pots during the bright, warm days of late spring and summer. When doing this, though, exercise some caution. In general, succulents with small, delicate leaves or with leaves that are coated with a decorative white powdery bloom should not be left out in the rain. More resilient plants, such as agaves, can safely be left in a sunny outdoor spot throughout the warmer months.

Always grow succulents in a well-drained potting mix to prevent root rot — even if strict control is kept on watering. Special cacti/succulent soils can be bought, but it is better to mix your own, since in that way you will know it contains an adequate measure of sand or perlite.

Natural clay pots and containers tend to look more in keeping with the desertlike character of succulent plants than plastic ones. Both types are perfectly suitable, however, and plants grown in plastic containers often need even less watering. Grow species that branch from the base or eventually form broad clumps in shallow boxes or azalea pans for a more balanced shape.

▶ **Rocky landscape** Miniature gardens replicating the natural habitats of succulents can make arresting focal points. Here, string-of-beads *(Senecio rowleyanus)* tumbles trailing stems over a plant tray; the tiny gray-green leaves are perfectly beadlike. A maroon-tipped sempervivum looms over an ornamental rock, at whose foot a miniature succulent with bright pink flowers nestles.

◄ **Tiger aloe** A popular succulent, tiger aloe *(Aloe variegata)* rarely exceeds 1 ft (30 cm) in height. It produces offsets that form a spiky clump. They can be removed and potted up singly.

◄▼ **Century plant** Agaves are dramatic foliage succulents with rosettes of tough sword-shaped leaves. The century plant *(Agave victoriae-reginae)* forms a wide clump of dark green, white-striped, spiny-tipped leaves.

▼ **Jade tree** The glossy-leaved jade plant *(Crassula ovata)* eventually forms a small, branching tree. During early growth, it can share a container with tiny succulents, such as *Lithops*.

BOTTLE GARDENS

**First developed in the Victorian era, the practice
of growing houseplants in enclosed glass containers is
both attractive and beneficial to plant health.**

Many tropical plants and the majority of ferns require more humidity and constantly higher temperatures than can be provided in the home. Chiefly foliage plants, they flourish in filtered light and the steamy atmosphere of tropical jungles.

Such conditions can be difficult to re-create in the home. On a large scale, botanical gardens build huge hothouses to simulate jungle conditions; on a smaller scale, closed plant cases — bottle gardens and terrariums — can provide similar microclimates. A closed plant case is in effect a mini-greenhouse: moisture from the soil condenses on the inside of the glass and runs back down, so the air and roots never dry out. Smoky and dusty air is also

kept away from the plants so leaf pores never get clogged and the plants are protected from drafts and sudden fluctuations in air temperature.

Bottle gardens
Narrow-necked, clear glass bottles of various sizes make handsome containers — the only restriction being that the neck must be wide enough to let small plants through. Large carboys are especially good for bottle gardens, often having a neck wide enough to put your hand through. Plastic bottles and tanks can be used, but condensation tends to build up on the inside of plastic and hide the plants; condensation runs off glass more readily.

When growing ferns and waxy-leaved plants, you can insert a stopper in the neck of the bottle to maximize humidity. However, with flowering plants or other soft or hairy-leaved plants, whose foliage is damaged by water drops, leave the neck open.

Choose small, slow-growing plants, such as miniature ferns, small-leaved ivies, fittonias, marantas, and for "ground cover," the mossy selaginellas, which need constantly moist conditions and rarely survive for long outside a bottle garden or terrarium.

If the bottle garden is to be viewed from all sides, set taller plants in the center. Choose from slow-growing cultivars of calatheas, dieffenbachias, and dracaenas. The brilliantly colored earth stars (*Cryptanthus* species) are also ideal for bottle gardens and plant cases. These small bromeliads, only a few inches high, make marvelous centerpieces. Their vivid leaf patterns show up best through clear glass.

Plan the arrangement before placing plants in the bottle *(see also pages 159 –162).* Ensure that small plants are not hidden behind taller ones and are not too cramped — bank up the potting soil toward the back of the bottle to create a tiered effect.

Flowering plants are not usually suitable for a bottle garden, since they have a short season of interest, then look nondescript; besides, deadheading is impossible. It is best to select plants with colored leaves to provide highlights. Add pebbles or bark chips around the plants to improve the visual appeal.

Water the plants by hand with

◀ **Plant cases** Glass containers of many shapes and sizes are suitable for bottle gardens. Old-fashioned candy jars, fish tanks, wide-necked bottles, and carboys are all excellent, provided the glass is clear, not colored. Moisture-loving foliage plants thrive in the enclosed, humid atmosphere and will need a minimum of attention.

capillus-veneris)
Watermelon peperomia (*Peperomia argyreia*)

Colored foliage
Aluminum plant (*Pilea cadierei*)
Arrowhead vines (*Syngonium podophyllum* cultivars)
Belgian evergreen (*Dracaena sanderana*)
Caladiums (*Caladium* cultivars)
Cretan brake fern (*Pteris cretica* 'Albo-lineata')
Crotons (*Codiaeum variegatum pictum* narrow-leaved cultivars)
Dumbcanes (*Dieffenbachia maculata* cultivars)
Earth stars (*Cryptanthus* species)
Ivies (*Hedera helix*, small-leaved variegated types)
Mother-of-thousands (*Saxifraga stolonifera* 'Tricolor')
Mosaic plant (*Fittonia verschaffeltii argyroneura* 'Nana')
Polka-dot plant (*Hypoestes phyllostachya*)
Ti plant (*Cordyline terminalis*)

◄ **Victorian terrarium** Suited to the elegance of a room full of antiques, this sort of terrarium offers the advantages of a bottle garden, but allows much better air circulation if one or more panes are left unglazed. Such a terrarium is easier to plant, and it is simple to adjust the arrangement as plants become larger.

Here, an ivy tumbles from one side, breaking up the symmetry of the terrarium. Color is provided by pink-tinted mother-of-thousands and a polka-dot plant. A green moss fern forms a delicate, contrasting backdrop.

a mist sprayer and, if necessary, clean the inside of the glass with a piece of sponge attached to a wire or stick. Place the bottle in good light — the glass reduces the amount of light inside the bottle considerably — but not in direct sunlight. The display will be self-supporting for several months. When plants become too large, replanting is often the best solution.

Terrariums

Terrariums were developed from the "Wardian" case, invented by an English physician, Nathaniel B. Ward, a century and a half ago. He was experimenting with caterpillars and discovered by chance that a fern spore had germinated in one of the stoppered jars. Further experiment showed that certain plants would grow indefinitely in sealed glass containers. The "Wardian" cases he designed greatly increased our collection of tropical plants, since the closed cases made it possible to bring home sensitive species on the decks of sailing ships.

Ward's terrariums, popular in the Victorian era, were often extremely ornate. A similar sealed container can be made from an ordinary fish tank, with a cover made to fit closely over the top.

Unlike bottle gardens, terrariums have a portable canopy of glass or plastic panes with metal glazing bars, which can be easily lifted off. This allows the cultivation of a wider range of plants, since it is easy to replace overgrown specimens and to move flowering species in and out.

Although plants can live for years in sealed cases, condensation does cloud the glass, so some ventilation is preferable. Here again, terrariums have an advantage over bottle gardens, as you can remove or open some of the panes of glass either permanently or for a few days when the glass becomes clouded.

A brass-framed or leaded-pane terrarium is expensive, though with care, such a container will last a lifetime. Cheaper all-plastic or alloy-framed terrariums are popular but have less charm.

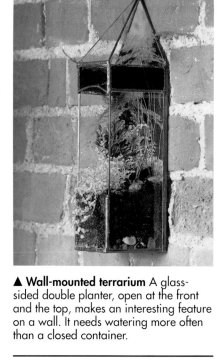

▲ **Wall-mounted terrarium** A glass-sided double planter, open at the front and the top, makes an interesting feature on a wall. It needs watering more often than a closed container.

Neither glass nor plastic glazing transmits all the available light to the plants inside the terrarium, and some natural sunlight is also lost through the room windows. All terrariums must therefore be placed in a bright spot — but out of direct sun, which will cause the glass to steam up.

Do not try to encourage quick growth by overfeeding; the fertilizer in most potting mixes is sufficient to last for several seasons. After that period of time, use half-strength houseplant fertilizer every 6 months only. Once a balanced environment has been established inside a terrarium, it should not need watering for several months or even years.

All of the plants recommended for bottle gardens are suitable for growing in terrariums. Small trailers and climbers can also be included if the terrarium has open sides. Orchids thrive in a terrarium, but generally flowering plants are more liable to rot in this enclosed, humid environment than foliage plants. Avoid cacti and succulents, which prefer dry conditions.

◄ **Traditional terrarium** Mossy selaginellas and small-leaved baby's tears *(Soleirolia)* thrive in the moist environment of a partially enclosed terrarium. The more vigorous ivies and tradescantias tumble through openings in the glass panes.

a plant pot on a waterproof tray or incorporated into an ornate wooden or stone plant stand.

PLANTING A BOTTLE GARDEN

The creation of a bottle garden demands dexterity and ingenuity, but the result is a long-lasting, low-maintenance houseplant display.

Just as model makers enjoy the challenge of building a ship inside a wine bottle, so many indoor gardeners derive a good deal of pleasure from planting and growing a miniature jungle inside a glass carboy or similar large bottle.

In fact, houseplants can be grown very successfully in almost any large transparent container, including wine magnums, old-fashioned candy jars, and other storage jars; even a goldfish bowl is suitable. Aquariums can also be used. They provide a better opportunity for "landscaping" the miniature garden and don't demand the same manual dexterity in planting.

Ideally, the glass should be crystal-clear, without any color, so that as much light as possible will pass through it. Pale green, very pale brown, or slightly smoked glass can be used, but the choice of plants is then restricted to shade-loving species. Dark green or dark brown glass bottles are not suitable for planting.

Clear plastic containers can be used for bottle gardens but tend to lack the charm of glass types. Plastic also has the unfortunate characteristic of allowing condensation to build up inside, so that the view of the plants is obscured. By contrast, glass is smoother and cooler, and condensation runs off more freely. However, the big advantage of plastic is that it won't shatter into sharp pieces if it is dropped — an important consideration if children or pets will be present.

The smaller the neck of the container, the more difficult it is to plant, but there is no real limitation on the proportions. Beginners to this art should choose a wide-necked container, but with experience many kinds of young plants can be inserted through a neck as small as that of a wine bottle. All you need are a few improvised tools, some patience, and a steady hand.

Apart from looking highly decorative, a bottle garden provides the extra humidity and protection that most jungle plants miss in modern houses, especially in winter. Such plants usually respond to this improved environment by growing better, often with more richly colored foliage.

Provided the plants are free from pests when they are first planted in the bottle, pest problems are almost nonexistent, especially if the bottle's neck is narrow or the mouth is corked. Fungal diseases and rots, whose spores are carried in the air or may multiply in the soil, can be a problem, but only if the bottle garden is neglected or overcrowded.

Miniature plants

Many garden centers and nurseries offer inexpensive young houseplants in tiny pots. However, check that they are well-rooted specimens and not merely new unrooted cuttings; inspect the drainage holes in the bottom of

▶ **Miniature bottle garden**
Moisture- and humidity-loving plants flourish in a closed environment. Their contrasting leaf colors, shapes, and textures become more vivid here than in the dry air of a living room.

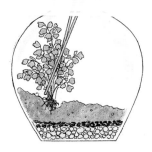

4 Lower the first plant into its planting hole. Either use two small bamboo stakes or pieces of dowel, or grip the root ball between two long-handled spoons. Then backfill the hole.

5 Repeat this procedure for plants at the sides and front of the bottle. You will find it easier to insert the lowest-growing species first, building up the planting in tiers.

6 As you get to the center of the planting, the foliage cover may make insertion of the last plant difficult. Wrap a paper tube around it, and slip it off after it is in position.

the pot for signs of roots. Or, try gently pulling the plant's main stem upward from the soil. If it is well rooted, there should be little or no movement.

A still cheaper way of obtaining plants for a bottle garden is to propagate your own. Seedlings or rooted cuttings can be used straight from the seed tray or propagating box. Gently shake extra rooting medium or seed-starting mix from the plants' roots — bare-rooted plants are easier to maneuver into a bottle without dirtying surrounding plants already in position.

Suitable cuttings — from your own stock of houseplants or from that of a friend — should be completely free of pests and diseases. Seed can be either collected or ordered from a mail-order nursery; in addition, seed companies often offer houseplant selections.

Preparing the bottle

It is important to clean the inside of the bottle thoroughly before attempting to plant in it. Dirt will impair the transmission of needed light through the glass, look unsightly, and possibly harbor troublesome fungal and viral diseases.

Rinse the inside of the bottle with detergent, then use cold water to flush it out. If the inside shows signs of mildew or mold growth on it, rinse with bleach and then water before the detergent. Bad stains on the glass can be removed by rinsing with cleaning solutions sold by wine-making supply companies. When clean, allow the bottle to air-dry in a warm place for a day or so.

Once it is dry, prepare the bottle for planting by covering the base with a 1-2 in (2.5-5 cm) deep layer of drainage material. Make

this by mixing a handful of charcoal chips with washed pebbles, none of which exceed ¼ in (6 mm) in diameter. The charcoal keeps any water that collects in the bottom of the bottle from turning foul.

Cover the drainage layer with fine gauze or fiberglass screening to prevent any soil from being washed down into it and clogging the pores.

Using a rolled-paper funnel or chute, add a 2-4 in (5-10 cm) layer of sterilized potting soil. This should not be a type that contains a lot of fertilizer and so encourages growth — the plants must grow slowly and remain compact, yet healthy. A mixture of 2 parts by volume of ordinary loam-based potting soil, 2 parts of coarse sand, and 1 part of sphagnum moss peat suits most recommended plants.

7 When all the plants are in place, lightly tamp the soil using a thread spool wedged on the end of a dowel. As you work, make sure that none of the leaves are buried.

8 Any remaining bare patches can be filled with fresh moss, pieces of wood bark or cork, or pebbles. Use a wire hook to insert moss, and a paper or plastic tube to scatter pebbles.

9 Moisten the soil and foliage with tepid water, using a hand sprayer with a fine nozzle. If the soil is very dry, use a plastic tube and funnel to apply water directly to its surface.

10 Leave the bottle unstoppered for a few weeks until the amount of moisture condensing on the inside of the glass is minimal. When the moisture balance has equalized, insert a cork stopper.

HOME-MADE TOOLS

plastic funnel and tube for watering

sponge wired to a stake

spoon wired to a stake

spool wedged onto a stake

wire loop

fork wired to a stake

scalpel wired to a stake

Unless you plan to view the bottle garden from all sides, bank the soil up toward the back, so that a tiered effect can be created more readily.

Planting
Select attractive plants in a range of sizes — taller but slow-growing ones for the back or center; shorter, compact ones for the front or edges and for ground cover. Also choose plants with a range of colors, shapes, and textures, which also complement each other.

As a general rule, avoid including flowering species in the plant grouping, since they usually have only a limited season and may be difficult to replace or deadhead. This does not mean that bright colors are excluded — there are many plants with striking colored leaves to choose from, and these give an attractive year-round display.

For the actual planting process you will need a number of special tools. These can generally be made from ordinary household spoons and forks, thread spools, and stiff wire, such as a heavy copper wire — each attached to a small bamboo stake or a length of dowel. Unless the neck of the bottle is wide, *never* try to squeeze your hand inside to plant or tend the garden. It may get stuck. It is also important to warn children of this danger.

It is best to begin by inserting plants close to the edge of the bottle and then work toward the middle. For a tiered planting effect, begin at the back, then fill the sides and front before completing the center.

Low-growing plants should always go in before the taller ones to minimize the danger of bruising their leaves. With rounded jars and bottles, remember that there is more available headroom for taller plants in the center of the container than at the sides. Plants that have their leaves squashed against the glass look unsightly, and the leaves may rot if they are permanently wet with condensation.

Use a long-handled spoon to smooth the surface of the soil, then make a hole for the first plant. Remove the plant from its pot and shake or tease away any excess potting mixture from its roots. Holding the plant's root ball gently but firmly between two long-handled spoons — or simply between two sticks (like chopsticks) — lower it into the hole. Use two spoons or dowels to gently pack the soil over the roots and keep the plant upright.

driftwood. Alternatively, press small pieces of moss into the gaps. These will soon spread in the humid atmosphere and provide an attractive ground cover.

Spray the bottled plants with a fine mist of tepid water. Aim to get the soil evenly moist but not wet. If a lot of water is required to moisten the soil, add it with a plastic funnel and tube.

Finally, if necessary, clean off any soil or plant debris from the sides of the bottle, using a piece of sponge attached to a dowel or a length of stiff but flexible wire. Set the bottle garden in a bright spot near a window but not in direct sun.

Care

During the first few weeks after planting, water vapor will escape slowly through the neck of the bottle. Excess moisture will also condense inside the bottle. The correct humidity level is reached when there is just the slightest trace of condensation on the inside of the glass. A lot of condensation indicates that the soil is too wet; none at all suggests that it is too dry and that more water should be added. Wipe off excess condensation with a sponge attached to a dowel.

When this fine moisture balance is achieved, insert a cork stopper in any broad-necked bottle. Bottles with narrow necks may be left open. Remove the stopper for a few days from time

3 Sever dead or diseased shoots, leaves, and flowers as soon as they are seen. Use a scalpel blade or razor blade fixed to the end of a dowel. Remove the prunings with a wire hook.

4 Remove dead plants or any that have become overgrown or unsightly by twisting a wire hook into the root ball and lifting the crown upward. Replace with a new plant as before.

to time to allow some fresh air in. A sealed bottle should need watering only very infrequently, but an open one must be given a sprinkling occasionally to prevent the soil from drying out.

Once a balanced internal environment has developed, the bottle garden needs little further maintenance. Dead leaves, flowers, whole shoots, or entire plants must be removed immediately to avoid rotting. This is best done by using an improvised long-handled cutting tool consisting of a razor blade or scalpel blade attached to a thin dowel with wire or adhesive tape. Severed plant material can be extracted from the bottle with a wire hook.

Unless the plants seem stunted, discolored, or otherwise unhealthy, fertilizing bottle garden plants is not recommended, since it will encourage excess growth,

swamping the display. If necessary, apply half-strength liquid houseplant fertilizer directly to the soil via a funnel and tube.

Terrariums

Terrariums or glass cases provide similar growing conditions to bottle gardens, but since the environment inside is not usually so tightly sealed, the potting medium dries out more quickly and humidity is lower. Terrariums thus require more frequent routine maintenance.

The planting procedure is the same as for a bottle garden, but you won't need such specialized tools — most terrariums have removable panels or unglazed sections through which you can work unhindered. The choice of plants for a terrarium need not be as limited as for a bottle garden because replacement is easy.

EYE-CATCHING BONSAI

The ancient Oriental skill of growing woody plants in tiny containers can produce an exciting range of miniature trees and shrubs.

The art of bonsai aims to duplicate all the characteristics of a mature and shapely tree or shrub in a miniature plant, which can be moved indoors for a short-term but stunning display.

The technique involves confining the plant to a small container — a shallow dish or bowl — by pinching back the top growth and pruning the roots throughout its life. A bonsai must be trained carefully in order to create the individual charm of a gnarled and twisted mature forest tree.

Most trees can be grown as bonsais, but those with imposing shapes and small leaves give the best results. Both conifers — firs, cedars, hemlocks, junipers, pines, and spruces — and broad-leaved trees — beeches, birches, hornbeams, maples, oaks, and zelkovas — are great favorites. The broadleafs look particularly fine in fall when many color brilliantly. Flowering and fruiting species such as crab apples, quinces, and cherries are also suitable.

Bonsais require constant care and attention. Plants must be watered according to weather conditions, container size, season, and leaf type. And because the restricted roots soon dry out, bonsais must be watered often much of the year. They must also be sheltered from desiccating strong winds. Bonsais are not strictly houseplants — the best place for them is outdoors on a patio, terrace, or balcony. They can be brought indoors when they are in full display, but must be moved outdoors again within a week or so. Indoors, they must have as much light and fresh air as possible. Stuffy and poorly lit rooms are not suitable.

Growth styles

Experts recognize three major classes of bonsai — single-trunk plants, multiple-trunk plants, and multiple-plant groupings. Single-trunk plants are trained into different forms:

❏ Formal upright — branches grow uniformly in all directions from a straight trunk.

❏ Informal upright — usually an S-shaped trunk with branches radiating from the outer curves.

❏ Slanting — branches grow in several directions from a leaning trunk.

❏ Windswept — branches grow from one side only of an arching trunk.

❏ Literati — branches restricted to the top third of a subtly twisted and slanting trunk, with relatively little foliage.

❏ Broom — upright trunk with branches spreading out like an upended besom broom.

❏ Umbrella — upright trunk with a broad crown.

❏ Weeping — upright or slanting trunk with pendent branches.

❏ Cascade — pendent trunk hanging over the edge of the container, similar to trees growing out from a vertical rock face.

❏ Semicascade — near-horizontal

◀ **Windswept bonsai** Almost a century old, yet no more than 2 ft (60 cm) tall, this miniature Chinese juniper has been carefully trained to mimic the windswept contours normally associated with buffeted hillside trees.

◄ **Formal upright** Japanese maples are among the most beautiful of trees suitable for bonsai culture, especially in fall when the foliage turns bronze and yellow, then orange, then intense scarlet. The branches of the formal upright style are elegantly layered, setting the foliage off to its best advantage.

► **Bonsai shrub** Normally bushy shrubs, such as red-fruited cotoneasters, can be trained into small, treelike bonsais with a gnarled elegance.

▼ **Weeping miniature** An antique Chinese pot enhances the Oriental theme of a weeping willow. As bonsais, willows produce masses of foliage and need constant trimming.

trunk, characteristic of trees growing by a lakeside.

❏ Exposed root — roots form the lower part of the aboveground tree.

❏ Root over rock — tree standing on a rock with roots spreading across its face.

❏ Rock-grown — tree rooted in a crevice in a craggy rock.

❏ Driftwood — sections of trunk and branches carved and stripped of bark to look like driftwood.

Shaping the basic style must begin while the plant is still a seedling or cutting, but the characteristics that give each bonsai personality develop and are enhanced as the plant matures.

Buying bonsais

Bonsai trees and shrubs are often sold by garden centers and nurseries, but since training takes many years, the price is high. When buying such a plant, make sure that it is healthy and hasn't been on display in a hot, dry spot for long.

You can save money and gain satisfaction by growing your own bonsais from seeds or cuttings — although a tree will take 10 to 50 years to develop its full character.

Basic cultivation

Bonsais need fresh air, nutrients, light, and water. In summer the soil in their small and shallow containers dries out extremely quickly, so they need watering daily or even twice a day during hot spells. Broad-leaved species can die within days if they are left unattended. At each watering saturate the soil, applying water from above until it runs out of the drainage holes. In spring and fall, keep the soil slightly moist. Don't water in winter unless there is a prolonged dry spell.

Grow bonsais in full sunlight. Shade encourages weak, spindly growth. However, some light shade in early afternoon in mid-summer helps to keep the leaves from scorching in the hot sun.

A good general soil mix consists of equal parts by volume of sphagnum peat, sand, and loam. Add extra sand for pines and use an acid mix for azaleas.

The dwarf habit of bonsais is not achieved by starvation. They actually need more regular feeding than other container-grown plants, since the soil provides little nutrition. Dilute liquid fertilizers to half their recommended strength to avoid burning exposed roots, but apply at twice the normal frequency.

In spring and early summer use a high-nitrogen fertilizer; in mid- to late summer use a high-potash fertilizer to induce fruiting and flower bud initiation and to harden the wood. Water before applying fertilizer. Special bonsai fertilizers are available, but ordinary houseplant feeds are equally suitable, if properly diluted. After repotting or after root pruning, postpone feeding for a few weeks.

Maintain humidity, especially when plants are indoors; stand the pots in a tray of moist pebbles.

Propagating bonsais

Bonsai plants can be grown from seeds, cuttings, or layers.

Seeds can be collected and sown. Alternatively, tree seedlings often appear in your own garden, and these may be lifted and potted up. The digging up of seedlings

BONSAI STYLES

Plants can be allowed to develop their natural, but dwarfed, growth form, or artificially induced shapes can be produced to mimic the stunting and aging processes of the extremes of nature.

1 Cascade
2 Multitree
3 Windswept
4 Slanting/exposed roots
5 Root over rock
6 Informal upright

seeds to a depth equivalent to two or three times their diameter. Germinate them in a cold frame outdoors. Some seeds may take up to a year to germinate, but dormancy can be broken by placing the seeds in a moist plastic bag in a refrigerator for a few months prior to sowing. When the seedlings are large enough to handle, pot them up individually. **Cuttings** are a slightly quicker source of actively growing plants. For deciduous trees, softwood heel cuttings taken in early summer to midsummer are the most successful. Evergreens are best grown from hardwood cuttings taken during the growing season. **Air layering** produces small rooted trees very quickly.

Choosing containers
A wide selection of special bonsai pots is available. They are mostly stoneware and usually glazed. Porcelain containers are much more expensive.

Improve drainage by placing a shallow layer of gravel or clay shards in the bottom of the pot before filling it with soil mix.

Shaping and pruning
You can use conventional small pruning shears, pruning knives, and household scissors for pruning bonsais, but enthusiasts may prefer to buy special bonsai tools. Gouging tools, chisels, and other small carpentry tools are re-

well-spaced branches.

To remove entire branches, use concave branch cutters or pruning shears, which give a clean cut flush with the trunk. Regularly trim other branches to the desired length, cutting close to and away from any buds. Use your finger and thumb to rub out unwanted buds.

The best time to prune is during dormancy. Begin by pruning poorly shaped branches as well as those that are inappropriately positioned for the desired form. Then shape the plant by selecting surplus branches and snipping them off. The goal is to produce branches that taper evenly from trunk to tip.

Wire is used to create curving or contorted shapes that rarely occur naturally. To force young shoots into the desired shape or position, tie them with wire until they are woody enough to remain rigid — up to several years. Wiring is best done in early summer when growth is most flexible.

Use wire that is thick enough to overcome the plant's natural springiness, but not so thick as to be obtrusive or stifle the plant. Never use ferric wires, which will rust. Instead, use copper or aluminum wire. Toughen copper wire before use by heating it to a high temperature in a fire. Aluminum wire remains more pliable than copper wire and does not oxidize so readily.

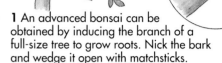

1 An advanced bonsai can be obtained by inducing the branch of a full-size tree to grow roots. Nick the bark and wedge it open with matchsticks.

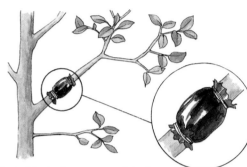

2 Tie black plastic around the branch and pack moist sphagnum moss around the wound. Secure the rooting medium by tying the top of the plastic.

3 When the branch is well rooted — after 6 to 12 months — remove the plastic. Sever the branch, cutting just below the roots, and pot it.

REPOTTING AND ROOT PRUNING

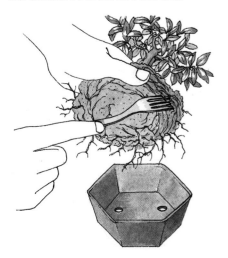

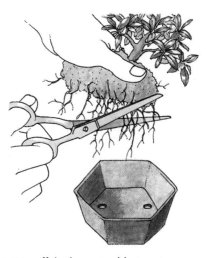

1 Every 1 or 2 years, or when pot-bound, remove the bonsai from its pot. Using a small fork, tease away the old soil and loosen the congested or spiraling roots.

2 Trim off the longest, oldest roots, reducing the root ball to such a size that it will fit back into the original container with enough space all around to take a little fresh potting soil.

3 If the tree is top-heavy, support it temporarily by looping string around the trunk and threading it through the pot's drainage holes. Add drainage material before repotting the plant.

Other methods of shaping branches include tying them to the pot with string, in the style of guy-ropes, and weighing them down. However, these techniques may result in branch breakage. **Root pruning** and repotting must be done every 1 to 2 years to ensure that the bonsai does not choke itself to death in its tiny pot. (Old trees need repotting after about 10 years.) Unlike most pot-grown plants, bonsais should not be moved into larger ones. Instead, make space for fresh soil and new, fibrous roots by pruning the old roots.

Remove the plant from its pot, pick off some of the old soil, and tease out the roots. Cut off the excessively long roots, then repot and water. Unstable trees can be tied in to the pot's drainage holes to keep them upright.

Leaf pruning aims to reduce the leaf size of broad-leaved species, to encourage twiggy growth, and to improve fall colors. In early summer or midsummer, use fine scissors to cut off unwanted leaves where the stalk joins the leaf; do not damage the growing bud at the base of the leafstalk. A second flush of smaller leaves will then appear.

Never leaf-prune weak trees, and don't do it for more than two consecutive summers. Build up the plant's strength before leaf pruning by applying fertilizer. Flowering plants should never be leaf-pruned.

Pinching back the growth tips is another form of pruning, used mainly for scaly-leaved conifers, including many of the junipers. Using your fingers, gently pull off new growth buds, taking care not

to damage the tips. Never slice off the buds with a knife.

Needle-leaved evergreens, *Juniperus rigida,* for example, can be pruned in a similar way. As new growth begins to elongate in spring and late summer, pinch the center of each tuft.

Special techniques
Each of the various growth types requires individual treatment over a period of many years — no two bonsai plants are the same, and personal taste will influence your approach.

Informal upright style is one of the easiest to achieve, since it

ROOT OVER ROCK

When planting, sit the base of the trunk in the crotch of a suitably shaped rock. Drape the roots over the rock, anchoring their tips in the soil. Wire down until stable.

WIRING TRUNKS AND BRANCHES

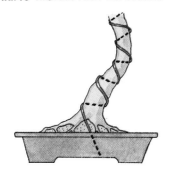

1 Train the trunk into curves by binding it with wire. Anchor one end, then twist the wire firmly but not too tightly in a spiral up the trunk. Leave it in place for a year.

2 Bend branches similarly. Anchor the wire to the trunk or to a nearby branch. Never wrap it across leaf nodes. Remove wire in fall to avoid scarring the bark.

branches from the viewing side than from the back of the tree to create a feeling of depth. Also remove any branch that overshadows the one below.

Slanting style requires the trunk to lean at about 45° from the vertical. Wire the trunk in place until it is firm and woody. Check the wires each year, rewiring if necessary to avoid strangling the tree bark. Encourage slightly exposed roots on the side away from the angle of lean, to create a visual sense of stability.

Windswept style is achieved in the same way as the slanting type, but cut out all branches on the "windward" side. Naturally windswept trees frequently have ripped and broken branches, some of which may have been severed completely, leaving only a jagged stump.

To counterfeit this on a bonsai, select an unwanted but otherwise healthy branch and make a cut about halfway through the wood, slanting away from the trunk. Then, pulling toward the trunk, snap off the branch by twisting and tearing it, leaving a rough end. Don't clean up the bark or wood surrounding the wound, but treat it with Bordeaux mix to prevent disease — after a year or so of natural healing, the stump should resemble genuine wind damage.

Root over rock style drapes a bonsai's gnarled roots over a

rock. This takes many years to achieve and demands extra care, but the final effect is rewarding. Maples, beeches, and junipers respond particularly well to this style.

Begin by encouraging a seedling tree — or one grown from a cutting — to develop long roots by planting it in a deep container. In 3 to 6 years, when these roots have formed, lift the small tree and tease out the roots.

Select a piece of rock that has fissures or a rugged surface that the roots can grip. Drape the long roots over the rock and bind them to it with wire. Then plant the tree and the rock together in a bonsai dish, burying the ends of the roots in the soil around the sides. Leave the root-over-rock planting undisturbed for at least 5 more years before repotting.

Multiple-trunk bonsais fork into two, three, or more separate trunks at or near ground level. Grow and train the tree in the same way as an informal upright, but prune it carefully to avoid

▲ **Bonsai collection** A group of mature and young bonsai trees creates an unusual focal point on a sheltered patio. They need outdoor conditions and plenty of light.

crossover of branches between each trunk. One of the trunks should be allowed to dominate the others in height and scale. Multiple-trunk bonsais can often be obtained quickly by air-layering a forked branch.

Group plantings can be made to look just like miniature dense forests, or with the inclusion of a bare space, they can resemble an open landscape. This style can make use of immature trees which lack suitable characteristics to form specimen plants.

You can grow a group planting in the same way as a formal upright. The trees' roots become entwined, and the group can be lifted from the pot as one. Don't try to separate them when repotting, unless one dies or becomes unsightly.

EASY-TO-GROW AIR PLANTS

**Air plants, as their name suggests,
live on air alone and will thrive in almost every
home with minimal attention.**

The term "air plant" applies to a small and very specialized group of bromeliads belonging to the genus *Tillandsia*. These unusual plants have two features in common: they have little or no root system, and they absorb most or all of the water and food they need through their leaves. Air plants range in size from tiny lichenlike plants to immense leaf rosettes, though the smaller ones are the most suitable as houseplants. Their native habitats range from humid tropical rain forests to arid deserts.

Air plants' survival is due to a mass of minute scalelike growths on the surfaces of the leaves, which extract needed moisture from humid air and nutrients from floating particles of dust. These scales give all tillandsias a grayish or silvery hue. Unlike other plants, they do not need soil for anchorage or for a food and water supply, so they can be mounted to almost any surface.

Sometimes nurseries and florists supply air plants attached to pieces of bark or gnarled wood, coral, or decorative seashells. This practice probably stems from the fact that most air plants resemble, to some extent, sea-dwelling organisms — especially sea anemones. Pieces of lichen are frequently used to conceal the adhesive material. The effect is eye-catching, and air plants mounted in this way form an interesting link between living plant displays and purely ornamental objects.

The best-known air plant is *Tillandsia usneoides*, or Spanish moss. It consists of threadlike stems covered with silvery scales that are, in reality, minute leaves. In the wild, this virtually rootless plant hangs from trees and rocks in long, tangled festoons. Spanish moss, therefore, is not used as a conventional pot-grown plant. Instead, indoor gardeners attach a few sections of the tangled mass to a small piece of cork or bark, tying the fine stems on loosely with monofilament fishing line and hanging the bark on a hook.

As with most bromeliads, the air plant rosette generally flowers only once and then gradually dies, but this process takes several years. Offsets are produced from leaf bases, and these may be detached and used for propagation or can be left in place after the withered old rosette has finally been removed.

Air plants do best in bright but filtered light. They grow year-round if the temperature is kept reasonably warm, but they will not tolerate cold conditions. Although water is needed in tiny amounts, it is advisable to mist plants regularly, especially in winter, when indoor air is dry. Avoid placing air plants over a radiator or other heat source, and don't mount them near fabrics or furnishings that might be damaged by misting. Apart from these minor limitations, air plants can be displayed almost anywhere — they can even be stuck to mirrors and glazed tiles.

◀ **Air plants** Although the true flowers of air plants are short-lived, the bracts enclosing them remain attractive for much longer. The yellow bracts of *Tillandsia fasciculata* 'Tricolor' contrast well with the gray, mauve-tinted leaves.

▲ **Artistic tillandsia** The display of
tillandsias demands some creativity.
Try to match the form of the plant with
the shape of the mount.

▼ **Driftwood plants** The curious leaf
arrangements of *Tillandsia filifolia* and
diminutive *T. ionantha* are complemented
by driftwood. Lichen adds to the charm
of the arrangement.

INSECT EATERS

Needing animal matter to supplement their diet, carnivorous plants are fascinating to grow in the greenhouse or home.

▲ **Sundew plants** Insects are attracted to the foliage of sundews *(Drosera),* which is covered with stalked, sticky reddish glands. A leaf slowly wraps itself around the creature, which is unable to escape from the glue and is then slowly digested. Plants are rarely more than 6 in (15 cm) tall.

Carnivorous plants are different from all other plants in their feeding habits. They have adapted to environments in which certain nutrients, such as nitrogen, are deficient in the soil. More in character with animals than plants, these curious species trap small insects and other creatures and digest them to acquire the missing nutrients. Enzymes secreted onto the ensnared creatures dissolve their bodies, and the resulting "soup" is absorbed directly into the tissues of the plant trap.

There are two types of traps. In passive traps, insects drop into some form of pit while in search of nectar. Examples include the jungle pitcher plants (*Nepenthes* and *Sarracenia* species), which produce large jug-shaped receptacles filled with water. Some pitchers have hinged hoods or lids to cover the trap; all eventually drown their prey.

Active traps have touch-sensitive triggers that cause a special leaf organ to clamp shut around visiting insects. The well-known Venus's-flytrap has hinged, two-lobed traps that are edged with long spines capable of rapid closure. Sundews operate similarly, but instead of confining their prey in a small prison until they die and can be digested, these small bog plants glue unsuspecting insects to their folding leaves with a sticky secretion. Sundews are also known as living flypaper!

Traps are often brightly colored; in addition, many carnivorous plants produce unusual flowers that attract insects. The dainty European butterwort, for instance, bears streptocarpus-like blue-purple flowers in summer. And sarracenias produce striking red or greenish-yellow nodding flowers, whose drooping petals form another type of trap — this time for capturing pollinating insects. Even if they are caught, the insects often successfully escape uninjured to pollinate the next flower.

Most insect-eating plants have special cultural needs. Use a free-draining yet moisture-retentive potting mix. A 50-50 mix of sphagnum peat and fine sand is suitable, or choose an acidic potting soil containing vermiculite. Plastic pots are best, since they retain more water. Stand each pot in a saucer partly filled with water. Don't use tap water — carnivorous plants hate the lime and chlorine found in most water supplies. Instead, water well with rainwater or distilled water.

No fertilizer is required, but unless your home is plagued by flies, drop tiny pieces of meat or cheese (or dead flies) into the traps occasionally. Grow in normal room temperatures in a bright spot, but out of hot sun.

▼ **Insect trap** Pitcher plants, such as the *Nepenthes* below, have leaves shaped like a pitcher, often with a hinged lid. These fill up with water, into which a digestive enzyme is secreted. Small insects, attracted by the brightly spotted coloring of the trap, crawl inside and then drown.

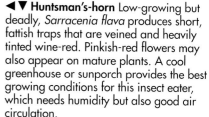

in hot weather.

◄▼ Huntsman's-horn Low-growing but deadly, *Sarracenia flava* produces short, fattish traps that are veined and heavily tinted wine-red. Pinkish-red flowers may also appear on mature plants. A cool greenhouse or sunporch provides the best growing conditions for this insect eater, which needs humidity but also good air circulation.

▼ Venus's-flytrap Native to the Carolinas, Venus's-flytraps are the most fascinating of all carnivorous plants. Their spiny-armed "jaws" spring closed when an insect touches a tiny trigger hair on the inner surface of the hinged trap. The rapid action can be fired by touching the hairs with the point of a pencil.

ACKNOWLEDGMENTS

Photo credits
Anaglypta ltd 114; Arcaid (R. Einzigt) 109; Biofotos 171 (t), 172 (bl, br); Guy Bouchet 10 (r); Linda Burgess 10(l), 44-45 (t), 55; Camera Press 35 (t); Brian Carter 131; Eric Crichton 43, 44 (tl), 45 (tr), 46 (tl), 59, 67, 75, 87, 106 (b), 115, 133, 134 (tl), 139, 149 (tl), 168; Arnaud Descat 135, 136 (b), 146, 149 (b); Eaglemoss/John Suett front cover; Garden Picture Library (Lynn Brotchie) back cover, 36 (b), (Linda Burgess) 4-5, (Brian Carter) 154 (br), (Mayer/LeScanff) 36 (t), (Perdereau/Thomas) 159, (J S Sira) 148 (b); Robert Harding Picture Library 6, (IPC magazines) 83; Annet Held 128 (b); Jan den Hengst 127; Jacqui Hurst 164 (bl); Insight (Linda Burgess) 141, (Michele Garrett) 50 (t); Patrick Johns 71, 79; Lamontagne 9, 11, 13, 50 (br), 51, 52, 91, 124 (tl, b), 125 (t), 136 (t), 137, 140 (tl, b), 142 (t), 151, 172 (t); Andrew Lawson 99 (b), 149 (tr),
169, 170 (t); Maison de Marie Claire 29, 95, 107, 110 (tl), 121, 153; Philippe Perdereau 126 (br); Photos Horticultural 2-3, 14, 17, 33, 35 (b), 37 (l), 54, 99, 104, 125 (b), 126 (tl, tr), 132 (tl, b), 140 (tr), 143 (l), 144, 150, 154 (tl, b), 163, 164 (tl, tr, br), 171 (b); Annette Schreiner 118 (b), 124 (tr), 142 (br), 152, 158, 170 (br); Harry Smith Collection 20, 31, 37 (r), 63, 116 (tl), 155, 156 (b), 157, 170 (cl, bl); Jean-Paul Soulier 50 (bl); Elizabeth Whiting and Associates 46 (b), 116 (tr), 123, (Karl-Dietrich Buhler) 106 (tl), 122, 130 (tl), 132 (tr), 138, 142 (bl), (Michael Crockett) 46 (tr), (Michael Dunne) 45 (b), 106 (tr), 111, 112 (tl, b), 117, 118 (t), 119, 129, 130 (tr, b), 134 (b), (Andreas von Einseidel) 128 (t), (Geoffrey Frosh) 105, 120 (br), (Clive Helm) 34 (tr), (Frank Herholdt) 110 (tr), (Neil Lorimer) 108 (c), (Michael Nicholson) 108 (t), (Orbis Library) 21, (Spike Powell) 113, (Jerry Tubby) 108 (b), 112 (tr); Worldwide Syndication/Strauss 148 (t); 100 Idées 47, 48 (br), 49.

Illustrators
Sylvia Bokor 16 (tr), 19 (bc); Elisabeth Dowle 18, 19 (tl, tc, tr, bl, bc), 20, 64-66, 72-74, 147, 165-167; Christine Hart-Davies 1, 12, 14, 16 (tl, bl, br), 22-28, 30-32, 34, 38-42, 56-58, 60-62, 68-70, 80-82, 84-86, 88-90, 92-94, 96-98, 100-102, 160-162; Claire Wright 158.

Index compiled by Sydney Wolfe Cohen

Reader's Digest Production
Assistant Production Supervisor: Mike Gallo
Electronic Prepress Support: Karen Goldsmith
Quality Control Manager: Ann Kennedy Harris
Assistant Production Manager: Dexter Street

Book Production Director: Ken Gillett
Prepress Manager: Garry Hansen
Book Production Manager: Richard Mangini
U.S. Prepress Manager: Mark P. Merritt